St Kitts

Cradle of the Caribbean

Second Edition

Brian Dyde

CARIBBEAN

First published 1989
Second edition published 1993

Published by THE MACMILLAN PRESS LTD
London and Basingstoke
*Associated companies and representatives in Accra,
Auckland, Delhi, Dublin, Gaborone, Hamburg, Harare,
Hong Kong, Kuala Lumpur, Lagos, Manzini, Melbourne,
Mexico City, Nairobi, New York, Singapore, Tokyo.*

ISBN 0 – 333 – 56932 – 6

Printed in Hong Kong

A catalogue record for this book is available from the
British Library.

Front cover photograph: The Circus, Basseterre |MICHAEL BOURNE|
Back cover photograph: The Fortress, Brimstone Hill |MICHAEL BOURNE|

*To the Woodley Family
and the memory of Angela James*

| Contents |

| Maps |

Maps drawn by the author

| Acknowledgements |

I should like to record my gratitude to those who have assisted me in gathering material this book. Phyllis Mayers and Vanta Archibald (the Public Librarians of St John's and Basseterre, respectively) were exceptionally helpful. Lionel Trotman, Meloflect Bass, Denzil Jones, D.L. Matheson and 'Moonlight' Roberts all provided useful information and statistics. I owe particular thanks to Julienne Hendrickson, Ralph Saunders, May Woodley and Lorna Edwards for giving me, over the years, valuable insights into modern St Kitts and the Kittitian character.

| 1 |
By any other name . . .

St Christopher is a Caribbean island. As one of the Lesser Antilles it forms a link in the chain of islands which separates the Caribbean Sea from the vastness of the Atlantic Ocean. At the same time it is one of the few that does not have an Atlantic coastline. The waters of the Caribbean and the Atlantic mingle some thirty-five miles to the north, along an invisible line between the islands of Barbuda and Saint Barthélemy. St Christopher is surrounded by the warmer, bluer and more benign waters of the Caribbean. Standing on the windward side of the island, with others in sight to the north and east, one does not get that 'standing on the edge of the world' feeling which is experienced on one of the eastern capes of say, Antigua or Guadeloupe, when watching the Atlantic rollers thundering in to the shore. The north-east coast of St Christopher receives its fair share of rough seas, but it is *Caribbean* surf formed by the breaking of *Caribbean* waves which pounds up the beach or smashes on the headland. The swell which produces such waves may still have been generated by a storm a thousand miles away in the middle of the Atlantic, but those last thirty-five miles make all the difference. To look to seaward in any direction from St Christopher is to view the Caribbean. The island is not unique in this respect but it is something which adds, like its unusual shape and singular history, to its distinctive character and charm. The fact that it is known to the rest of the world by a colloquial abbreviation of its name only adds to its individuality.

It is not known when St Christopher started to be called St Kitts but it certainly dates back to sometime in the eighteenth century. Since then the shorter name has taken the place of the correct title on seemingly everything but official documents: even the modern postage stamps have dispensed with the full name. The inhabitants always refer to the island as St Kitts, and to themselves as 'Kittitians'; and so they are known by anyone else in the world aware of their

Sunrise over St Kitts (MICHAEL BOURNE)

1

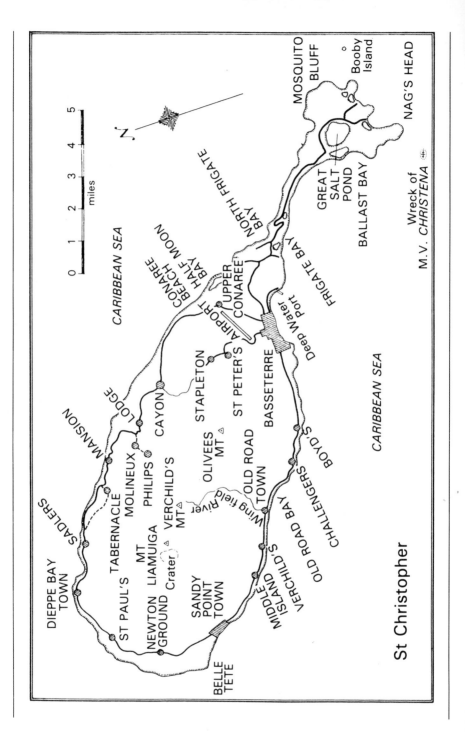

St Christopher

existence. The entry for St Christopher in most guidebooks and encyclopaedias usually consists of the words 'See St Kitts'. So universal is the use of the diminutive that the country of which the island forms one half is, to quote from the Constitution, 'a Sovereign and Democratic State which may be styled Saint Christopher and Nevis or Saint Kitts and Nevis'. This brings us to another peculiarity of the island.

St Christopher rises from a submerged bank which it shares with two other islands. To the north-west is the small island of Sint Eustatius across an eight mile stretch of water called The Channel. This is one of the Netherlands Antilles and as such nothing at all to do with its larger neighbour. To the south-east across the two mile width of The Narrows is the island of Nevis. This has been very much associated with St Christopher since the earliest days of European colonisation. Regardless of their close proximity, of their interdependence and interrelationship as separate British colonies for over two hundred years, and of their union as a single colony more than a century ago, the two islands could well be out of sight of each other for all their inhabitants have progressed towards a true sense of common nationality. In this respect they are not alone in a region of the world where a number of small independent States have been formed each consisting of two or more islands, but they are certainly at odds with multi-island States elsewhere. A New

The island of Nevis seen from Frigate Bay on St Kitts
(MICHAEL BOURNE)

Zealander, for instance, is first and foremost a New Zealander whether he lives in the north of North Island or eight hundred miles away in the south of South Island. But not so here, where a Nevisian remains a Nevisian and a Kittitian a Kittitian even though they live in sight of each other and have shared a common citizenship since 1882. That they stare at each other across a narrow stretch of water which was the scene of one of the worst and most heartrending disasters in the history of the State adds great poignancy to the parochialism. The ramifications of their mutual antipathy (if this is not too strong a word to describe the mostly good-natured rivalry tinged with suspicion that exists between them) will interest historians and sociologists, not to mention the local politicians, for the foreseeable future. However neither Nevis nor the reasons for the differences which exist between that island and St Christopher are the subject of this book. Readers who would like to know more about the other half of the State should turn to the companion volume by Joyce Gordon, *Nevis: Queen of the Caribbees*. The remainder of the present book is devoted to the island which from now on, like everyone else but the legal draughtsman or the pedantic historian, we can refer to as St Kitts.

It is an island altogether different from its neighbours. For a visitor to St Martin, Antigua or Saint Barthélemy the main impression must be that of an island devoted to tourism and to serving the needs of the, mostly North American, tourist. In other islands – Sint Eustatius, Anguilla, Barbuda, and even Nevis to some extent – there is a distinct feeling of timelessness and of very little happening, for tourists or anyone else. St Kitts is unlike any of them. It is a *working* island, and while tourists are just as welcome here as in any of the other islands they will soon realise that life goes on here much as it does in their own countries. In islands such as Antigua or Anguilla, which are mostly covered with thorn scrub, the visitor may be forgiven for enquiring about what the majority of people do for a living: there is little excuse for such a question in St Kitts.

The growing of sugar-cane has been the mainstay of the economy since soon after the island was colonised. Sugar has dominated life from the seventeenth century until today, affecting not only the face of the island but the social patterns, habits and outlook of the people, whether directly concerned in its production or not. This single crop economy has had its detrimental effect, helping to stultify independent thought and encouraging acceptance of the status quo.

Disasters, whether natural or man-made, seem always to have had a much greater effect here than that caused by similar events elsewhere. More lives have been lost and more damage done in individual accidents and catastrophes than the size of the population at any time has warranted. At the same time the dominance of sugar has had some beneficial aspects. The role of agriculture in a small island's economy, which has been rejected or degraded in so many of the islands round about, has retained its importance. An 'economic diversification programme' with a 'three-way development strategy', consisting of the expansion of tourism, the establishment of light industries, and the introduction of new crops (in that order), is mooted frequently and at length by politicians in all the eastern Caribbean islands. This has far more meaning in St Kitts where a large proportion of the labour force is still engaged in agriculture and, more importantly, working on the land is not considered demeaning.

For most visitors such things will have little relevance or interest. The tourist seeking a quiet Caribbean vacation, and all that goes with it, can be excused if she shows no curiosity about an island's economic problems; she may well, after all, have come to escape for a while those besetting her own country. However, much of the pleasure to be derived from such a vacation comes from getting to know the people. The inhabitants of the small islands of the eastern Caribbean have an enviable reputation for genuine friendliness and hospitality. It can be argued that in some of the islands it is becoming increasingly difficult for visitors to get to know anyone not connected in some way with the tourist industry, and so gain real insight into a particular country. This is far from the case in St Kitts. The visitor who wants to will have no trouble in meeting people with no connection with hotels, restaurants, souvenir stores or any other part of the 'tourist industry'. Given genuine interest and goodwill on his part, and by observing the local standards of courtesy in such simple matters as the exchange of greetings appropriate to the time of day, he will soon get acquainted with some of the least pretentious and more hard-working people in the region. It will help to have some idea of how the Kittitians came to be what they are today, and a sizeable part of this book is given over to their history. But before seeing how St Kitts has treated and affected the people we should look at the island itself.

| 2 |
The fertile island

Location and formation

St Kitts is about two hundred miles to the south-east of Puerto Rico and four hundred miles north of Trinidad. Like its immediate neighbours Nevis and Sint Eustatius it is of volcanic origin, and all three islands can be viewed as the exposed bits of one large mountain rising from the floor of the Caribbean Sea. They were raised above the surface of the sea by a series of enormous and violent volcanic upheavals which took place millions of years ago. In between these outbursts the older rocks sank back into the sea and became covered with marine limestone, only to be disturbed by the next series of eruptions. Today St Kitts is almost entirely made up of volcanic rock, but with some limestone outcrops raised high above sea-level here and there. The water surrounding it, over the submerged bank which joins it to Nevis and Sint Eustatius, is generally less than one hundred feet deep. On the south-western side, this bank extends only a short distance away from the coast, but on the opposite side of the island it stretches for two or three miles offshore in places. Once the edge of the bank is reached the seabed falls rapidly to depths of 1500 feet or more.

The main part of the island

St Kitts is about 68 square miles in area, with the very distinctive shape of an Indian club or a paddle, lying in a north-west to south-east direction. Most of it is made up of a range of mountains which rise steadily in height from east to west. They culminate in a dormant, though not completely extinct, volcano which until 1983 was called Mount Misery. When the island became independent in that year the peak was re-named Mount Liamuiga – this being the name by which the island was known to the Amerindian inhabitants before its discovery by the Europeans. The top of a jagged cone-shaped pinnacle on the eastern side of the crater is the highest point on the island at 3792 feet.

The mountains are divided into three parts, each separated from

6

Mount Liamuiga from the east coast (MICHAEL BOURNE)

the next by a col. The one called Phillips Level, between Verchild's Mountain in the centre of the island and the peaks which form the South East Range, has a trail connecting one side of the island to the other. Apart from this footpath the only communication between the various communities on opposite coasts is by the road which circumnavigates the whole mountain range. The slopes are steeper on the windward north-eastern side, but all around they have been cleared up to about one thousand feet above the sea. Sugar-cane is grown from the coast up to seven or eight hundred feet, and above that the cleared land is used for growing ground provisions or for grazing. From the edge of the cleared area to around the 3000 feet level the mountains are covered with forest. Above this height the vegetation is equally thick but much more stunted. The lush vegetation gives the island a most attractive and inviting appearance. From a few miles out at sea it is difficult to tell the cultivated land from the forest and St Kitts looks much as it always has done – a green island, the shades changing with the passing hours and the passing clouds, rising smoothly from a cobalt blue sea. The drifting clouds, which often obscure the mountain peaks for long periods, bring a constant supply of rainwater, and the volcanic soils are particularly fertile. Appropriately enough the Carib name *Liamuiga* is thought to have meant 'the fertile island'.

The long peninsula

The eastern end of the mountain range tails off into a broken pattern of low hills in the neck of the 'paddle' where it joins the 'handle'. These hills partly surround and divide the only large area of flat land on the island, containing the most fertile sugar-cane fields, the main town, the airport, and the principal tourist locality. The 'handle' itself is a long narrow peninsula of rounded hills ending in a wide triangle of higher hills surrounding a very large salt pond. One mile seaward of Mosquito Bluff, the easternmost point of St Kitts, is a steep-sided islet called Booby Island, uninhabited except for the seabirds which give it its name. The peninsula is very different in appearance from the rest of the island. The hills are the remnants of very old volcanic activity which took place long before Mount Liamuiga was formed. They have been greatly worn down and the action of the sea has had much more effect here than elsewhere on the island. The small bays with their white sandy beaches and the salt ponds behind some of the beaches are similar to those in the limestone islands of the eastern Caribbean. The hills with their coarse grassland, scrub and a few stunted trees are also very similar to those in islands like Anguilla or Antigua which are composed mostly of limestone. The entire peninsula, most unlike the rest of the island, is infertile and agriculturally valueless.

Vegetation

The natural vegetation is lush and varied on the main part of the island. Around the coast it consists of sea-grape trees and lots of herbaceous plants – especially the prolific morning glory vine – with various sedges and coarse grasses. The lower mountain slopes, above the cultivated areas, are covered with forest. The trees range from those useful for timber, such as mahogany, cedar, poui, lignum vitae and bamboo, to those bearing fruit like the orange, lime, mango, custard apple, sapodilla and soursop. Besides these there are many palm, casuarina, tamarind, calabash, banyan and bay trees, not to mention the ubiquitous coconut. Trees and shrubs grow in profusion in the many 'guts' – the deep, narrow defiles which carry streams and rivers during the rainy periods. The vegetation on the mountain

**Royal palms in St Thomas's churchyard,
Middle Island** (MICHAEL BOURNE)

St Kitts: cradle of the Caribbean

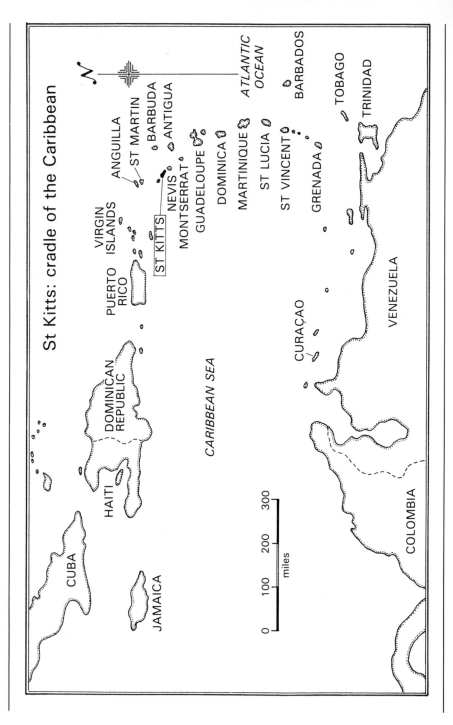

**Egrets are a familiar sight in St Kitts. At night they fly home
to roose in a favourite tree or mangrove** (CHRIS HUXLEY)

summits is just as dense as on the lower slopes but of a different
sort. There are no tall trees but only low bushes, sedges, bromeliads
and ferns. Orchids are common, as are aroids, arums and lianas. In
days gone by the approach roads to the various estate houses were
lined with royal palms, and rows of these majestic trees can still
be seen here and there among the cane fields. Around the salt ponds
and some of the bays of the peninsula there are large areas of
mangroves, while the hills above them support various kinds of
acacia and cacti.

Animal and bird life

The wild life of the island is very limited. Before the first European

11

settlement it probably consisted of little more than a number of rodents such as rats, mice and agouti, a few reptiles – iguana, lizards and snakes – and several kinds of bats. There were also large numbers of wild pigs, presumably descended from animals imported by the early Amerindian inhabitants.

The coming of the Europeans brought about drastic changes. The very edible wild pig and the rather less appetising iguana were soon hunted out of existence, and before the end of the seventeenth century a species of monkey had been introduced. The French, who as will be seen occupied half the island for nearly a hundred years, are usually blamed for the presence of vervet (or 'green') monkeys. It is assumed that the present population of these animals (which

The green vervet monkey, of which there are around 35 000 on the island (CHRIS HUXLEY)

may well exceed the human population in numbers) is descended from one or two brought to the island as exotic pets from Africa. They are ground monkeys, without prehensile tails, which live in groups of thirty to fifty, feeding off fruit, insects and young shoots. The male is much larger than the female, but neither makes a good house pet. Like another imported animal, but not quite to the same extent, they are thought of generally as a nuisance. The other import was the mongoose, brought to St Kitts from Jamaica in 1884 to keep down the rats and snakes in the cane fields. As in every other island where it was introduced for the same reason it is now considered to be a pest. Having made the agouti extinct and more or less wiped out the snakes it is now a scourge of the remaining wild life as well as of chickens and small domestic animals.

The visitor will be made far more aware of birds than any wild animals. The bird life, as might be expected in such a mountainous island, is not only reasonably extensive but varies from one part to another. Around the coast the brown pelican and the frigate bird are the most common. In built-up areas small birds like the yellow-breasted bananaquit, starlings, ground doves and the unmistakable hummingbird are always to be seen where there are flowering shrubs and trees. The salt ponds attract herons, kingfishers, ducks and coots, with the bird population rising appreciably during the migratory season. Bird life is most prolific in the mountains. Besides the more common ones seen at lower levels it also includes various hawks, quails and pigeons. Although St Kitts may not be ranked very high in any ornithologist's list of the world's, or even the Caribbean's, best bird-watching locations, anyone whose interest this is and who is prepared to walk into the remoter parts of the island will not be unrewarded.

Climate

The main reason for the arid appearance of the south-eastern part of the island is the lack of fresh water. The average rainfall in this area is less than 40 inches, compared with perhaps 150 inches on the mountain peaks. An average for the whole island is around 60 inches a year. The wettest months are from September to November and the driest between January and April. Most of the rainwater, because of the nature of the soil and the rock beneath it, quickly disappears below ground. Above the one thousand foot level in the main mountain range there are plenty of streams flowing constantly, but below that there is only one permanent river. The Wingfield River, which flows down the southern side of Verchild's Mountain, has never been known to dry up. Two other rivers flow for most of the year but dry up at the height of the dry season. The many other river beds named on the map are only filled with water from time to time. For an island in the tropics with such a high average rainfall St Kitts has a remarkably fine climate. The normal daily temperature near the coast is about 80°F (27°C) with a relative humidity which is usually not very high. The island is kept cool by the trade wind which blows with great constancy from a direction between north-east and south-east for most of the year.

Together with all the other islands in the eastern Caribbean St Kitts is threatened by a hurricane from time to time. The regional meteorological authorities have determined a 'hurricane season' which lasts from July to November, but the threat is at its greatest in August and September. No one need be deterred from visiting during these months or any other part of the 'season': very adequate warning is given of the approach of one of these tropical storms and sound precautions are taken to protect life and property.

Earthquakes

The island, again like all its neighbours, suffers from the occasional earthquake or earth tremor. While the former can cause considerable damage and distress, and the latter – if it continues for any length of time – a great deal of unease, neither is any more frequent here than in any other place in an earthquake zone. A particularly severe earthquake occurred in 1843, which was felt not only in St Kitts but in all the other islands from St Thomas to St Vincent. A contemporary account gives some vivid details of its effect in St Kitts:

> . . . *The stone dwellings and stores in Basseterre, the capital of the island, fearfully shook and rent, – some of the finest, but a mass of ruins, and others rendered unsafe. The north and south vestibules of the parochial church of St George were severely injured, as well as the walls of the main building, which in some places were rent from top to bottom. The clock stopped at half-past ten, the time the earthquake commenced;*

many of the mural monuments which adorned the interior of the church were also destroyed . . . One large dwelling, situated in the square . . . fell a complete prey to the violence of the rockings. The entire side walls fell down, which striking upon a horse-stable beneath, buried the unfortunate animals in the ruins. Some of the private dwelling-houses were completely gutted, nothing remaining of them but the exterior walls. The gaol was so shattered, that the prisoners had to be removed, and accommodated for the night in the hospital building. The square was crowded with a concourse of persons of every age, sex and condition – pride, rank, power, were alike forgotten – as upon bended knees, or with clasped hands, and pallid lips, they invoked the aid of that Great Being . . .

The estates in the country suffered greatly; steam-engines, windmills, boiling-houses, proprietors' dwellings, etc, the labour of many years, were in one moment levelled with the ground . . . Upon one estate, report said, that three negro-houses sank into the earth; and in the vicinity, the ground opened, and a pool of water . . . was formed. In the neighbourhood of Sandy Point . . . the earth also opened, and vomited forth from its secret depths fumes of sulphureous vapour . . . From Mount Misery . . . a long spiral cloud of white smoke was seen to ascend during the time of the earthquake; and the sulphureous spring situated in its centre is said to have overflowed its bounds.

At Johnstone's, or French River, a melancholy catastrophe occurred. It is a spot chosen by the washerwomen of Basseterre as the scene of their necessary avocations; and upon the eventful morning of the earthquake, about ten of these females were busily employed in washing, in a natural basin, (formed by huge rocks) at the moment of the shock taking place. Seven of these women fortunately escaped by flight; but the three, who were exactly underneath the cliff, met a more melancholy fate. At the commencement of the awful commotion, an immense rock parted from this cliff, and fell into the stream below. The affrighted females fled from the scene of danger; but, alas! the increased oscillations of the earth caused it to rebound with fearful velocity, and striking against a larger rock, it split into three or four pieces, and thus dealt destruction to each of the poor panic-stricken women!

Earthquakes which have taken place since then have not been as severe, and such 'awful commotions' probably present less danger in St Kitts than in many other places which suffer from them. At least here there are no high-rise buildings or extensive conurbations to aggravate the effects of a shock. All in all, as has been recognised by the island's inhabitants and visitors throughout its history, the threat posed by earthquakes or hurricanes is far outweighed by the splendid climate, the fertility of the land, and the beauty of the whole island. While the last of these attributes may not have meant much to the early European colonisers, the first two – as will be seen —most certainly did.

| 3 |
The mother colony of the West Indies

The island was inhabited long before any Europeans arrived in the New World. An Amerindian people known as Arawaks entered the Caribbean from South America about two thousand years ago, and by AD 1500 had occupied all the islands as far north as The Bahamas and as far to the west as Cuba. They were followed at a much later date by a more warlike people called the Caribs. By the time the first Europeans reached the West Indies the Caribs had driven the Arawaks from all the small islands to the east and south of Puerto Rico. One of the islands they then occupied in some strength, on account of its rich soil and abundant water, was the one they knew as Liamuiga.

Carib petroglyphs (G W LENNOX)

Anguilla

St Martin

St Barthélemy

0 10 20 30 40 50 60
miles

SAN CRISTOBAL

Barbuda

SANTA ANASTASIA

SAN JORGE

SAN MARTIN

SANTA MARIA LA ANTIGUA

SANTA MARIA LA REDONDA

SANTA MARIA DE MONSERRATE

N

DESEADA

SANTA MARIA DE GUADALUPE

MARIAGALANTE

TODOS LOS SANTOS

DOMINICA

The islands named by Columbus in November 1493 on his second voyage to the New World

Martinique

Columbus and San Jorge

The island first entered recorded history on 12 November 1493. On that day Christopher Columbus sailed along the south-west coast, having spent the previous night at anchor off the south coast of the island he had christened San Martin, but which we know as Nevis. The larger island which now lay off his starboard beam he decided to call San Jorge. He did not land on either island but it seems likely that he would have seen signs that they were already inhabited by the same sort of people he had encountered a few days earlier in what is now Guadeloupe. Neither island retained the name he gave it. The inaccuracies of the first charts and maps made it difficult for later Spanish explorers to relate particular names to particular islands in this area, especially when they found yet more islands to the north. San Martin soon became Santa Maria de las Nieves (from which Nevis was quickly derived), and San Jorge was re-named San Cristobal (although this title had been given by Columbus to the present-day Saba, a little further to the north-west). The suggestion often heard that the famous discoverer named St Kitts after himself is a myth – as is the theory that he called the island by this name because it bore some fanciful resemblance to the legendary giant who carried the Christ-child over a stream.

Thomas Warner and the first settlement

Regardless of its name change the island remained a Spanish possession for over a century after its discovery. It was never settled as the early colonisers were much more interested in the Greater Antillean islands and the central American isthmus. The only interest the Spanish showed in this or any other island in the eastern Caribbean was in trying to prevent other European countries from establishing a foothold in the New World. The fact that St Kitts supported a sizeable Carib population may also have had much to do with their lack of interest.

Because of the Spanish monopoly of the Caribbean the first attempts by the British to establish a New World colony had to be made along the coast of South America between the mouths of the Amazon and Orinoco rivers. This region, now occupied by Guyana, Suriname and French Guiana, was known as the 'Wild Coast', not only because of the hostility of its inhabitants, but also on account of the nature of the coastline and the hinterland. One of the first

Fishing boats on the front at Basseterre Bay (BRIAN DYDE)

attempts to found a settlement, near what is now the border between Brazil and French Guiana, was made in 1620. It failed quickly and miserably, but two of the ships which had brought the settlers from England remained in the area. They were commanded by Captains Thomas Paignton and Thomas Warner. The former at some stage had visited St Kitts, and his glowing account of its attributes inspired Warner to take a look for himself, and this he did in 1622.

No one who has had the opportunity of approaching from seaward the coasts of Guyana (to take one example of the 'Wild Coast') and St Kitts will have any difficulty in understanding why Warner, once he had reached the island, stayed there for several months. Nor is it hard to imagine why he then hurried home to England to raise capital in order to start a settlement. For someone coming from months spent in a mosquito- and shark-infested anchorage in opaque, muddy water off a desolate shoreline of swamp and mangroves, inhabited by hostile Indians, inedible animals and a large variety of poisonous reptiles and insects, the appearance of St Kitts from a few miles offshore must have seemed paradisical. The luxuriant forest climbing from the water's edge up into the clouds; the island rising out of the bluest of blue seas; a secure anchorage in clear water within a few yards of the shore; flowing streams of fresh water from which the ship's casks could be filled; all must have made in indelible impression. Even the Carib inhabitants, of whom there were reported to be 'a formidable number', were welcoming and helpful – unlike the savages of the 'Wild Coast'.

Back at home Warner soon found a rich London merchant, Ralph Merrifield, ready to invest in his venture, and an aristocratic patron to introduce him at the court of King Charles I. The story is often repeated that Merrifield and Warner renamed the island, using the first syllables of their names, and calling it 'Merwar's Hope'. Although such a name was in fact coined (it appears in Warner's Royal Commission for the establishment of his settlement) it seems far more likely that it was intended as a business or trading name. The word 'Hope' was used in its now archaic sense meaning an enclosed piece of land, and 'Merwar's Hope' could well have been the name intended for the estate the two men intended to establish. Similar 'hopes' (Betty's Hope in Antigua and Good Hope in Guyana, for example) were soon to be established elsewhere which remain as estates to this day.

Accompanied by only a handful of settlers Warner left England in 1623 and arrived back at St Kitts on 28 January 1624. They landed halfway along the south-west coast and established themselves at the mouth of the island's only permanent river. They found a few Frenchmen had preceded them but, considering the size of the Carib population, it was thought prudent to let them remain: a sound short-term tactical decision no doubt, but one which was to have long-term repercussions. The Caribs, under a leader with a name which has been variously rendered as Tegreman, Tegreeman or Tegraman, continued to be well disposed towards the newcomers and both English and French set about clearing enough land to start planting tobacco. The following year Warner went back to England with the results of this first crop. This time he was able not only to induce a much larger number of settlers to return with him, but also to collect his commission from the King. This appointed him Governor not only of St Kitts but also of the nearby islands of Nevis,

Montserrat and Barbuda (mistakenly given in the royal document as Barbados), *'which said Islandes are possessed and inhabited only by Savages and Heathen people, and are not, nor at the tyme of the descovery were in the possession, or under the gouerment of any Christian Prince, State, or Potentate'*. On his arrival at St Kitts with the *'diverse of our subjects of this our Realme'* Warner found that more subjects of the French monarch had found their way there too.

A French privateer, Pierre Belain, Sieur d'Esnambuc, whose ship had been badly damaged in a fight with a Spanish vessel, called at St Kitts in October 1625 in order to carry out repairs. He and his crew were welcomed by the British settlers and allowed to clear enough land to grow their own tobacco crop. However, they were not welcomed by the Caribs who, as an eighteenth century historian put it:

> . . . *were willing enough to live peaceably with the Europeans who first landed there, and were upon the place when D'Esnambuc came thither; but, upon his landing, their boyez, or conjurers, telling them, in a general assembly met on purpose, that the foreigners were come to take away their country from them, and destroy them root and branch, it was resolved to massacre the English.*

The Caribs from other islands were summoned and hostile moves made against both the English and French. The two small communities united, drove off the invaders from the other islands and, early in 1626 '. . . *fell upon the most factious of the natives by night, killed them, and drove the rest out of the island.'* This cold-blooded massacre was to be only the first of a long series of disasters brought upon the people of St Kitts. For a beautiful island offering so much to enhance life, its inhabitants were to suffer grievously from both man-made and natural calamities during the next three centuries.

Division of the island

The Carib threat having been eliminated d'Esnambuc then repeated Warner's flying visit to Europe in order to find sponsors and to raise capital for a proper French settlement. On his return with a group of settlers he and Warner drew up a formal treaty, dividing the island between them. The French Saint-Christophe consisted of the northern end of the island, called Capesterre, and the lowlands near the neck of the 'paddle', called Basseterre. The English St Christopher was the central portion between Capesterre and Basseterre. The peninsula was left as neutral ground with the salt ponds being for the use of both sides. The treaty was signed on 13 May 1627, and ratified at intervals thereafter until 1662. Although it provided for both parties to remain neutral in the event of war breaking out between England and France, and allowed various common rights, the treaty had limited value and certainly did not bring about any sense of unity. This was demonstrated within less than two years of its signing, when the island was attacked by a Spanish fleet in a last attempt to keep foreigners out of the Caribbean. The two sides failed to co-operate effectively in resisting the attack, had their settlements destroyed, and were forced to abandon the island. Fortunately the Spanish were in no position to occupy or defend their conquest and both lots of settlers soon returned. Each side then concentrated on its own affairs, clearing land, growing tobacco and ground provisions, establishing fortifications, and laying down the beginnings of permanent communities.

The name of the southern part of Saint-Christophe was soon adopted as the name of the town built by the French, on the edge

Old Road Bay (MICHAEL BOURNE)

of a large bay on the leeward coast. The bay itself, which afforded the best anchorage anywhere along this coast, inevitably became known as Basseterre Bay. The main anchorage for the English part was the smaller bay further to the north-west where Warner had landed in 1624. How and when this bay and the town which grew up on its shore came to be called Old Road is not known. A 'road' was the common seventeenth century term for an anchorage, but as this particular one remained the main landing place for British ships for the first hundred years of the colony's existence it is not easy to believe it was thought of as 'old' (implying there was a newer one elsewhere) during this period. Nor is it clear why the town, as the capital of St Christopher, was not given a proper name. After all, the settlers who left there in 1628 to colonise Nevis soon named their first settlement Jamestown, making it odd that those who remained in St Kitts should have been content with 'The Road' or whatever they called it at the time. Perhaps spurred on by Warner's colonising ventures – Antigua and Montserrat, as well as Nevis, had been settled by 1632 – d'Esnambuc sent parties of settlers to the islands to the south of Antigua. They failed to dislodge the strong hold of the Caribs on Dominica and St Lucia, but by 1625 both Guadeloupe and Martinique were in French hands. These acquisitions, both English and French, led on to other settlements. By the middle of the seventeenth century the former had claimed Barbuda and Anguilla, while the latter had gone farther afield and established themselves in St Croix, Saint-Barthélemy, St Martin, St Lucia and Grenada.

While all this colonising activity was taking place there were great changes in the mother colony. D'Esnambuc died in 1636 and was succeeded as Captain-General of Saint-Christophe by the Chevalier Lonvilliers de Poincy, who took up his post three years later. Warner died in 1648. By then he was a man of substance, knighted and much esteemed. That the terrible slaughtering of the original Carib population some twenty-two years earlier may not have been entirely to his liking can be judged from the fact that he left behind a son born to a Carib woman. He gave full recognition to 'Indian' Warner (as the son was known), and had him raised – with the understandable resentment of the boy's English step-mother – in his own home. Lady Warner's rancour saw to it that the cuckoo did not remain in the nest once her husband was dead; 'Indian' Warner was soon driven from St Kitts and died many years later in Dominica.

The number of settlers, English and French, rose very quickly in the early years. The land was not all that easy to clear and a lot of heavy manual labour was involved. Clearance started along the foreshore, making room to build huts and plant the first crops. Among the timber was a certain amount of logwood. This, after gold, had been the most valuable product found in the New World by the early Spanish explorers. It was processed for producing dyes and its importation into Europe was a major part of the Caribbean trade in the sixteenth century. By the time St Kitts was settled the demand had fallen off, and in any case the island's total supply was soon used up. The first cash crop was tobacco and this remained the chief product for many years. Production reached its height in 1638 when nearly half a million pounds were exported. Cotton was also planted and remained a useful crop throughout the seventeenth century. However, in 1648 a number of Dutch refugees from Brazil brought with them a new crop; one for which the island was ideally suited, and which was to change everything.

Sugar and slaves

The introduction of sugar-cane not only killed off the tobacco crop and changed the whole appearance of the island, but also brought about a complete social upheaval. Within twenty years of its introduction all tobacco production had ceased and many of the small farms had been assimilated into what were from now on to be called 'plantations'. What came to be known as 'the great clearing' started around 1650, and large tracts of forest disappeared to make way for sugar and cotton fields. At first the planters relied on indentured European labourers to carry out this work, but it was soon found to be more advantageous to use slaves brought from Africa. The indentured servants, at the end of their period of service, had difficulty in finding land of their own. Many, not having the wherewithal to buy land or much desire to continue labouring in the fields, became nothing but propertyless vagabonds. The large number that were Irish were seen as a threat to the security of St Christopher, it being correctly assumed that in the event of a war with France they would side with their fellow-Catholics. From about 1650 onwards many of the 'poor whites' left, to try their luck elsewhere in the Caribbean. As the planters continued to increase the size of their estates so the importation of slaves boomed. The population figure of 20 000 quoted by some authorities for St

Christopher in 1650 or even earlier seems much exaggerated. It may have appeared to an irate contemporary observer that the island was awash with impoverished Irish tatterdermalions, but it seems highly probable that an extra digit was tacked on to his estimate of their numbers for effect. The figures available for the mid-1660s, showing the population of the English part of the island as just over 3000 and that of Saint-Christophe as about 3300, with roughly equal numbers of blacks and whites on either side, seem much more realistic.

The end of Saint-Christophe

Amicable relations between the two sides lasted until 1666 when war broke out as a result of England and France taking opposite sides in the Second Dutch War. The French invaded the British part and gave the settlers the choice of either swearing allegiance to the King of France, or selling their property. As a result over four hundred transfers of property were recorded. When peace was restored in the following year this led to great difficulties, and it required four years of negotiating to achieve a complete re-transfer of the lands back into English hands. From then on there was little love lost between the two sides. The French occupied St Christopher again in 1689, but were driven out a year later by an invading force which landed at Frigate Bay, just to the east of the town of Basseterre. The French forces were pushed northwards and finally beseiged in a fort on the north-west coast. This was overlooked by a steep-sided peak about 800 feet high, which because of the strong smell of sulphur at its foot was called Brimstone Hill. The English dragged guns to its summit and soon bombarded the French into submission. The whole island then remained in English hands until 1697 when, under the terms of the Treaty of Ryswick, it was divided as before. No sooner had this been done than war broke out yet again between France and England. This time the English forces in the island were the stronger of the two; the immediate surrender of the French parts was demanded and obtained. Although a French fleet attacked in 1706 and landed troops who did a great deal of damage, the island was not surrendered and remained in British hands from then on.

Rawlins Plantation gardens (MICHAEL BOURNE)

Brimstone Hill from Bloody Point (MICHAEL BOURNE)

Under the terms of the Treaty of Utrecht signed in 1713 the French gave up all claim to the island, and Saint-Christophe went out of existence.

Considering the general state of affairs in Europe during the seventeenth century, when in any conflict the French and English invariably took opposing sides, it seems incredible that people from these two countries could ever have contemplated a permanent division of one small island between them. In spite of the treaty of 1627 the two sides were at war with each other for at least a quarter of the time they occupied St Kitts together. After about 1660, by which time both sides were well established and the growing of sugar-cane was becoming increasingly profitable, it seems more than likely that each was keeping a close eye to the main chance. The various conflicts between them in the second half of the seventeenth century certainly provide no example of anything other than the overriding desire of one side to evict the other. The reluctance of the English to give their main settlement a proper name should have been enough to warn the French from the beginning. It must have been obvious that Basseterre Bay was by far the best anchorage and that once the town of Basseterre was established it would come to dominate the life of the whole island.

That the two sides managed to live in peace for as long as they did probably owes much to the fact that St Kitts was used as a base from which to settle other islands round about. Surplus people and energy were directed outwards and not across the internal borders. By the time the English and French got around to disputing with each other for its possession the island had sent people off in all directions, and early Kittitians were to be found in all parts of the Caribbean. St Kitts well deserved the title given it by later historians – 'mother colony of the West Indies'.

| 4 |
A plantation colony

With the departure of the French after the signing of the Treaty of Utrecht a great deal of valuable agricultural land became available to the British. Some of it was given away soon after the island was unified but the majority was sold by auction in 1726. A proposal that a certain amount of land should be divided into small plots and made available to some of the poorer white families was ignored, and all of it was sold in large 200-acre lots at prices which only the existing wealthy landowners could afford. This put a stop to the growth in the number of peasant farmers, and further concentrated the arable land into sugar-cane plantations. This deliberate act fixed the pattern of life in the island from then on, creating an almost unbridgeable gulf between a small number of rich estate owners on one hand and a mass of very poor, landless workers on the other. As more and more of the poorer whites moved to other islands, and the supply of indentured labour dried up, the work-force was replenished by slaves.

Basseterre Bay from the Ocean Terrace Inn (MICHAEL BOURNE)

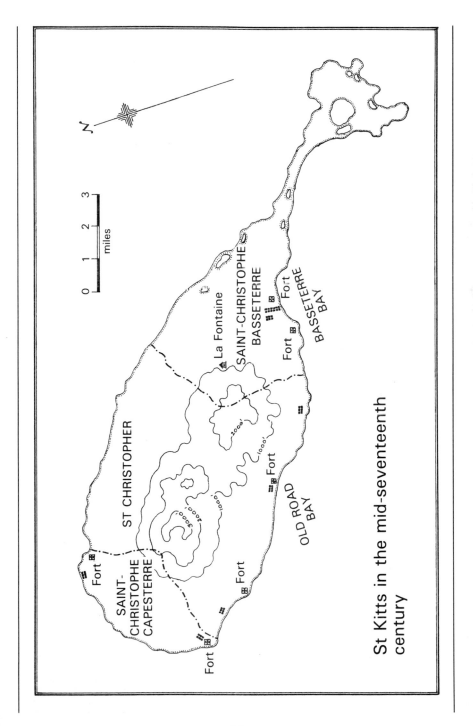

St Kitts in the mid-seventeenth century

The *Prince of Orange* tragedy

One day in March 1737 several hundred slaves from the 'Guinea Coast' in West Africa arrived in Basseterre Bay on board a vessel called the *Prince of Orange*. As was usual once the ship had anchored the slaves were released from their fetters and brought up from the hold. Before they could be landed and sold it was necessary to let them recover in the fresh air from the effects of the terrible Atlantic crossing, while they were given fattening foods and made to look presentable. During the first few days after the ship's arrival various people – the ship's agent, the slave auctioneer, a chandler – came to visit the captain, some accompanied by their personal slaves. After one such visitor had left the captain noticed *'a great deal of discontent among the slaves, particularly the men . . .'* This restlessness continued for the next few days until, in the late afternoon of 16 March, more than a hundred of the slaves rushed to the bulwarks and jumped into the sea. To the amazement and consternation of the captain and his crew, who saw the profits of their voyage about to disappear, once in the water the slaves made no attempt to swim ashore but rather made every effort to kill themselves. Thirty-three drowned themselves, while many more, having been forcibly rescued and then sold, died a day or two later. It was discovered afterwards that the panic had been caused by a slave belonging to one of the visitors. This individual, having a warped sense of humour and finding that he spoke the same language as the unsold slaves, had told them that once they were taken ashore their eyes would be put out and they would be eaten.

This horrific incident, although its main effect was on men who never actually became part of the population of St Kitts, encapsulates a tragic theme which has run through the life of the people of the island from the earliest times. The first known inhabitants, the peaceful Arawaks, were overrun and wiped out by the warlike, cannibalistic Caribs, who in turn were cruelly massacred by the first European settlers. African slaves were introduced from the very beginning but it was not until the early years of the eighteenth century that they started to outnumber the white population by any large amount. Thereafter, throughout the island's period of its greatest prosperity – lasting from about 1720 to 1780 – the number of slaves increased constantly until they outnumbered the whites by more than ten to one. The institution of slavery, with its debasing effects on the lives of blacks and whites alike, can be viewed as

Cutting cane (BRIAN DYDE)

the greatest disaster of all which befell the people of St Kitts; it influenced every aspect of life on the island for more than two hundred years.

Profits and wars

St Kitts was called the 'garden of the West Indies' in the early part of the eighteenth century and for its size was judged Great Britain's richest overseas possession. More and more land was taken over by cane fields and gradually the island took on the appearance it still bears today, with sugar-cane being grown all around the main part almost from the water's edge to seemingly halfway up the mount-ains. Within eleven years of the Treaty of Utrecht, out of a total population of 13 000, more than 10 000 were slaves; fifty years later there were less than 2000 whites and over 20 000 blacks. The reduction in the white population reflected the continuing concentration of land ownership into fewer and fewer hands. And as time went by many of these, by now, extremely wealthy individuals removed themselves from the island to buy or enlarge imposing mansions in Britain, while leaving their plantations in the hands of managers, agents and overseers. Sugar production rose steadily, from under 1000 tons in 1710 to over 10 000 tons a year by 1770.

The sugar plantations continued to make their owners large profits until the outbreak of the American War of Independence in 1775. Immediately the price of most things necessary to run a sugar estate started to rise. Once France declared war on Britain in 1778 communications with the island were disrupted and prices rose even higher. A French fleet attacked in 1782, troops were landed, and the fortress which by this time had been built on Brimstone Hill was besieged. After the capitulation of the fortress the French occupied the island until the end of the war in the following year. The French attacked again in 1805 during the Napoleonic Wars. Once again the garrison had to retire into the Brimstone Hill fortress, leaving the rest of the island in enemy hands for a while: the citizens of Basseterre avoiding having the town destroyed only by paying a sizeable ransom.

Peace and emancipation

By the time peace was restored between Britain and France in 1815 the heyday of the 'plantocracy' (a somewhat derisory term coined in Britain around this time for use, presumably, by those envious of the fortunes made in the West Indies, or by those critical of the ostentation displayed by many of the planters) was long past. Eight years earlier the Abolition Act passed by the British Parliament had made the slave trade illegal, and it was apparent that the emancipation of the slaves was only a matter of time. In addition sugar from beets was by this time being extracted successfully, and the development of national sugar beet industries in Europe was being encouraged.

During the early years of the nineteenth century the number of plantations was reduced to about one hundred and fifty. These belonged to less than ninety individuals, of whom less than one

This fine example of colonial architecture by The Circus now
houses a restaurant and art gallery (MICHAEL BOURNE)

quarter lived on the island. The majority of the estates were run
by agents who, while trying to meet obligations to owners living
thousands of miles away, were just as interested in maintaining their
own status and looking after their personal interests. Caught between
the absentee landowners' demands for profits, and the ever-present
manangers' demands for greater productivity, were the 20 000 or
so slaves. Even with the abolition of slavery in 1834 the indignities
and cruelties heaped upon the blacks were not at an end. A six-year
period of 'apprenticeship' for field workers was ordained 'to ease
the owners' distress'. In the event this lasted only four years and
by 1838 the entire population of St Kitts consisted of free men and
women – although of course some were freer than others. For the
ninety per cent who were black life did not improve all that much
to begin with. The agricultural land belonged to the plantation
owners and very few were willing to part with any of it, even for
housing. The freed slaves had little option in most cases but to
remain as workers on the estates they had once belonged to, living
in small, congested communities of tiny houses built on land they
had to rent. Only on an estate between Basseterre and Old Road,
called Challengers, was land for housing sold outright.

The island's legislature of course was dominated by the plantocracy, and members saw to it that their own interests were looked

Frigate Bay Beach (MICHAEL BOURNE)

after. Various Acts were passed binding the labourers to particular estates, with a schedule of punishments for absence from work, and restricting the sort of jobs which black people could undertake. A licence was needed to become a porter, a driver or a lighterman, for example, and these were issued sparingly. One effect of these restrictions was to make many of the workers, as soon as they could afford the passage, leave for another island where pay and conditions were better. This created a shortage of field workers and caused the estate owners to resort to the scheme which had operated two hundred years previously – the employment of indentured labour from abroad.

Indentured labour

During the 1840s about 1500 Portuguese workers came to the island, mostly from Madeira. In spite of their well-deserved reputation as excellent farmers and gardeners the kind of work they were given in the cane fields held no great attraction. Many returned home at the end of their period of indenture, while those that remained soon found more congenial employment in the commercial life of the island. Within a few years those who had settled had prospered, and by the late 1800s several had become estate owners themselves.

A similar scheme, involving Indians from the poorer parts of the sub-continent, brought about three hundred workers to St Kitts in the late nineteenth and early twentieth centuries. These too found it more beneficial, at the end of their contracts, to leave the island or to enter commercial life. Generally speaking, from 1838 onwards, it was difficult for any estate to get enough workers from amongst the black Kittitians. With a continual decrease in the value of St Kitts' sugar, in competition with both beet sugar and the produce of larger islands, working conditions remained poor and wages even poorer. By the last decade of the nineteenth century things were in a very bad way. Most of the villages which had come into existence by then were still tied to particular estates, after which many of them were named, each housing the estate's workers in poor and primitive conditions. The road system was so bad that there was little contact between the villages, or with Basseterre. Such a community was no place for anyone who did not, or would not, work on the adjoining estate. Basseterre was the only other place such people could go to, other than by emigrating, and the town's population increased steadily throughout the nineteenth century. By 1890 it housed half the total population of the island – a situation which has existed more or less ever since. During the same period, from 1840 to 1890, the island suffered more of the catastrophic happenings which have been such a feature of life in St Kitts

More disasters

The 'great earthquake' of 1843, which caused much damage to property as well as the deaths of the 'affrighted' washer-women at French River, was a natural disaster over which no one had any control. The outbreak of cholera which devastated the population eleven years later was something which was capable of being contained by the authorities. In the event nothing much was done or achieved. The disease, which is caused and spread by living in insanitary conditions, killed nearly 4000 people – about one sixth of the population. No one in the British colonial administration seemed unduly perturbed by the scale of the disaster. This perhaps was not unexpected; after all many thousands more British troops died of the same disease that year during the Crimean War, and there was certainly no Florence Nightingale to succour the victims in St Kitts.

Of those who died of cholera more than 1500 had lived in Basseterre, and this was the scene of the next catastrophe in 1867. The 'great fire' of that year started in a bakery, but soon spread to destroy five hundred houses and to make five thousand people homeless. The beneficial effect of this would not have been apparent to those who suffered, but it did allow parts of the town to be laid out and re-built in a more sensible fashion. The reconstruction had hardly been completed when the town was struck by the 'great flood' of 1880. During a single day in January of that year something like 36 inches of rain fell on the central part of the island. With such a deluge it is understandable how whole buildings were washed into the sea, but it is not quite so apparent why more than three hundred people should have lost their lives at the same time.

Each of these disasters affected, as they always do, the poorest sections of the community and those with the least resources to withstand them. It is difficult, in reading accounts of them, to find much evidence that those in authority – either on the island or in London – did much more than wring their hands helplessly while deploring the cost to the public exchequer that each one caused. The division of Kittitian society, created by 250 years of slavery which had ended only a generation or two earlier (and even in 1880 a fair number would have been born in slavery), had been driven too deep. It was a community organised along rigid lines, denying any semblance of equality between blacks and whites. In a more equable and caring society the havoc wrought by any one of these disasters would have led to at least a shake-up of the local administration, and a chorus of abuse from British colonial officials and parliamentarians. That they produced neither of these reactions is not surprising – even less so when, as will be seen, a comparable tragedy, which took place a hundred years later failed to dislodge a single member of the, by then, all black administration, or to produce anything but token sympathy from the British Government. The circumstances of this modern disaster will be recounted in due course, but first we should look at just how the island has been administered over the years.

| 5 |
From colony to country

The Colony of the Leeward Islands

The mixture of peoples, African, European and Asian, which formed the population of St Kitts by the last decade of the nineteenth century was governed in much the same way as their predecessors had been for the previous two hundred years. From the beginning the island had been associated in one way or another with some of its neighbours. By 1675 it was one of a loose federation of colonies, embracing all the British islands between the Virgin Island group and Dominica, styled the 'Leeward Islands'. This was an administrative title with no geographical foundation. Much to the puzzlement of succeeding generations of visitors to the region it is also a contradiction in terms. All the islands of the eastern Caribbean, from the Virgin Islands to Trinidad, formed for the early Spanish explorers the 'Windward Islands', as they all lay in the path of the prevailing easterly winds. The true 'Leeward Islands' are those which lie parallel to the north coast of South America between Los Testigos and Aruba. Be that as it may, the British sub-division of the true 'Windwards' has had an ineradicable effect on the maps of the region and St Kitts, like its neighbours, is still to the world at large a member of the Leeward Islands grouping.

These colonies were administered by a Governor-in-Chief or a Governor-General who, from 1698 onwards, lived in Antigua. St Kitts, like each of the other islands, was under the authority of a Lieutenant-Governor, who governed through a legislature consisting of a Council and an Assembly. The Council was made up of ten men chosen, invariably, from among the wealthiest planters and merchants. The twenty-four members of the Assembly were elected by freeholders from the various parishes into which the island was divided. The system never worked too well, as the Assembly was usually at odds with the Lieutenant-Governor and his Council, and all were often in dispute with the authorities in London. By the middle of the nineteenth century the representative system had fallen into such disrepute that twenty or more members of the Assembly were being elected by fewer than fifty electors; and out

39

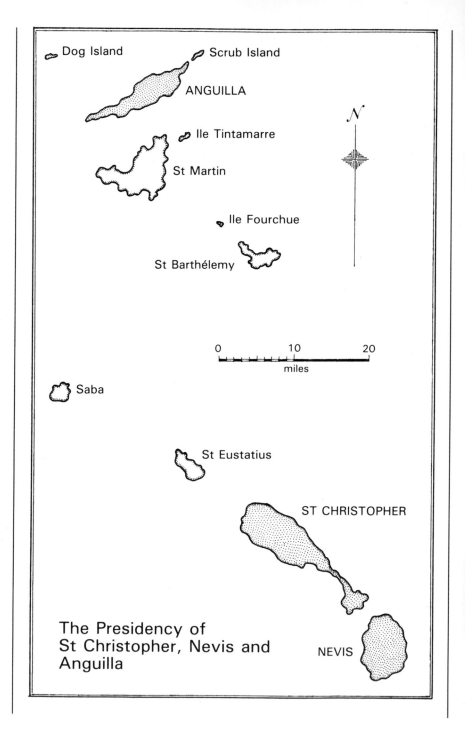

Dog Island

Scrub Island

ANGUILLA

Ile Tintamarre

St Martin

Ile Fourchue

St Barthélemy

Saba

0   10   20
miles

St Eustatius

ST CHRISTOPHER

The Presidency of
St Christopher, Nevis and
Anguilla

NEVIS

of a total population of 20 000 less than one per cent were eligible
to vote. In 1866 a single chamber legislature was introduced with
only twenty members, half elected and the other half nominated
by the Lieutenant-Governor. This made no difference to the way
the island was run or for whose benefit – the plantocracy still
remained in power.

The Presidency

Various reorganisations of the Leeward Islands took place during
the nineteenth century, but the two most important changes
occurred in 1871 and 1882. The earlier date saw the creation of
six 'Presidencies' within the group, each under an Administrator.
That of St Kitts was given authority over the smaller island of
Anguilla, some sixty miles away to the north. This was another
purely administrative decision on the part of the British government,
taken with no regard for the wishes of the people of either island,
but one which was to have considerable repercussions a century
later. In 1882, again for the purposes of 'tidying-up' the colonial
administration, and taking no account of local feelings, Nevis was
added to the Presidency of St Kitts. By this time the representative
form of government had been abolished and the Administrator ruled
all three islands with the help of wholly nominated Executive and
Legislative Councils.

This state of affairs lasted until 1937 when five places on the
Legislative Council were reserved for elected representatives – three
from St Kitts and one each from Nevis and Anguilla. Eligibility to
vote still depended on meeting certain property and income qualifications. As no more than about 1500 of the inhabitants of all three
islands could meet these qualifications it was no more than a nominal
step towards genuine representative government. But it was a start,
and the elections held in 1937 did see the entry into the legislature
of men not of the plantocracy. By this time the term 'plantocracy'
had long dropped out of use in Britain, and it is doubtful if it was
ever in common use in the West Indies. It has been revived in recent
years and is used frequently in modern Caribbean polemic writings,
where it ranks with such words as 'racist' and 'colonialist' as a term
of abuse. In the same way, the workers that these new members
of the legislature were elected to represent in 1937 had long ceased
to labour on a 'plantation', but were now employed on an 'estate'.

Middle Island Village (MICHAEL BOURNE)

Riots and representation

The return to some form of representative government was brought about at this time largely because of the growing unrest among the poor, landless and by far the biggest section of the population. The riots which took place in St Kitts in 1935 were part of a series that flared up at this time throughout the British West Indies. In every case they were caused by desperation – the poorest in each society reacting to the savage combination of grossly inadequate pay, bad working conditions and frequent unemployment, all made worse by the general world-wide depression of the 1930s. In St Kitts the riots produced immediate panic among the authorities; several lives were lost, and order was restored only after the calling in of the traditional British gunboat (in reality the cruiser HMS *Leander*).

The disturbances in the West Indian colonies between 1935 and 1937, besides forcing the British Government to introduce social reforms and to give the people of each island a greater say in their own government, also had another important result. One recommendation of the Royal Commission (which is always called the Moyne Commission, after the name of its chairman) which was set up to look into the causes of the unrest, was to strengthen local trade unions, or to encourage their formation where they did not already exist. In most islands the formation of such unions led rapidly to the creation of the labour-oriented political parties which dominate in the region today. In St Kitts the position was reversed. The Workers' League which had been formed in 1932 basically was a political party which, although successful in contesting every election from that of 1937 onwards, was fairly ineffectual when it came to industrial relations.

The estate owners, now appearing in an updated guise as the Sugar Producers' Association, had little difficulty in keeping their labour force in what they considered to be its place until 1940 when the St Kitts-Nevis Trade and Labour Union was formed. The leadership of this organisation was to all intents and purposes that of the Workers' League, and the two bodies continued in partnership from then on. The years of the Second World War saw a revival of the sugar industry. Demand increased and all controls on production and imports to Great Britain were lifted. The workers, through the efforts of their new union, were able to gain some modest improvements in their pay and conditions but, by the end of the 1940s, the lot of the majority of Kittitians was really little better than it had been ten or twenty years earlier.

Genuine reform and improvements started only after further changes were made in the way the island was governed. A new Constitution in 1952 introduced universal adult suffrage, a Legislative Council with a majority of elected members, and an Executive Council with three elected members. The St Kitts-Nevis Labour Party, which had grown out of the Workers' League, easily won all five of the island's seats on the Legislative Council in the first elections held under the new system. In 1956 the three elected members of the Executive Council assumed responsibility as Ministers for such matters as trade, public works, communications and social services. Four years later the position of Chief Minister was established and the total number of Ministers increased – placing more power and responsibility in the hands of elected representatives. An even greater change took place in 1967 when St Kitts, like all the other small British islands in the Eastern Caribbean, became an 'Associated State'. Under the terms of an agreement with Great Britain, the State of St Kitts-Nevis-Anguilla acquired full internal self-government. The Administrator was replaced by a Governor, the Legislative and Executive Councils were abolished and replaced by

a Senate and a House of Representatives. All members of the latter were elected by universal adult suffrage, and the State was governed by a Premier and a Cabinet drawn from the majority party in the House.

The loss of Anguilla

The incorporation into one State, under a Government in St Kitts entirely responsible for the internal affairs of the island, was not welcomed by the people of Anguilla. The island was nowhere near St Kitts, had never experienced the plantation system, and although poor did not have a large landless peasantry. With much justification Anguillans felt that they were treated as 'poor relations' by St Kitts, and could not see their lot improving as part of the new State. A rebellion broke out within a few months of the achievement of associated statehood and demands were made for 'separation and self-determination'. Subsequent events, which included the ejection of a British envoy, the landing of British troops and policemen, a fatuous raid by Anguillans on Basseterre, the carrying out of two referendums, the holding of four general elections, the drawing up of several Constitutions and the passing of various Acts by the British Parliament, dragged on for the next fifteen years. Eventually they led to Anguilla being severed from any connection with St Kitts, and to the island returning to its full colonial status under a British Governor in 1982.

The people of Nevis were possibly equally unhappy about the place of their island in the new State, but not to the extent of taking matters into their own hands. Their murmurings about secession were encouraged by an event which took place in 1970, and from which relations between the two islands still suffer.

The *Christena* disaster

Basseterre and Charlestown, the capital of Nevis, are in sight of one another, separated by barely twelve miles of water. This short passage, across what for all but the odd few days each year is an entrancing stretch of sparkling azure sea, between two of the most

Government House, St Kitts (previous page) (MICHAEL BOURNE)

pleasing islands in the Caribbean, has been made countless times during the past three and a half centuries. Among all the different ships and boats making the crossing there must always have been – since very early on – vessels engaged in providing a ferry service. In view of the ease and frequency of the crossing it is all the more tragic that one of the very worst disasters in the history of both islands should have happened in recent times to such a ferry. The accident, which was wholly preventable and the result of gross incompetence, caused grievous harm to the people of Nevis. By one of those terrible twists of fate, which no novelist would have dared to use in a tale about strained relationships between two lots of islanders, those responsible for it came from St Kitts.

The disaster happened in the afternoon of 1 August 1970. The ferry, named *Christena*, was a large motor-boat owned and operated by the Government. It was designed and licensed to carry 150 passengers. On the day of the accident some 330 people had been allowed on board. This almost unbelievable act of folly not only reduced the ferry's freeboard to a matter of inches, but also made her inherently unstable. The instability was compounded by the fact that manholes in the steering-gear compartment, well below the normal waterline, had been left open – effectively destroying the vessel's water-tight integrity.

Once the boat reached open water on its way from Basseterre to Charlestown it began to roll alarmingly. Water washed on to the upper deck, and much of it found its way into the steering-gear compartment. As the *Christena* entered The Narrows and encountered slightly higher waves, causing even greater rolling and producing panic among the passengers, she flooded up by the stern and rolled over. By this time, two hours before sunset, she was in about sixty feet of water and a little over one mile from land. Unfortunately the nearest point of land was the remote, uninhabited south-eastern headland of the long peninsula.

The life-saving apparatus proved to be useless, and the rescue and life-saving operations carried out by other boats (which arrived only shortly before nightfall) were uncoordinated and only partially effective. Altogether some 240 men, women and children of all ages were drowned. As the majority of them were Nevisians the death-toll was truly appalling, affecting nearly every family on the island. Something like two per cent of the population died; a figure which can only be appreciated if it is considered that a disaster of comparative size in the United States would have produced over one million dead.

The loss of the *Christena* had a traumatic effect on the three year old State, and influenced the internal politics of both islands from then on. To the outsider not familiar with the degree of fatalism found in the make-up of most West Indians it may seem surprising that there is no proper memorial in either island to those who died. The one which was erected in Nevis has been vandalised, while the smaller one which was put up on St Kitts has disappeared. The wreck itself, which lies on the direct track of the present ferry, is a popular venue for diving enthusiasts – having been turned it would seem into what can only be thought of as a macabre 'tourist attraction'. The disaster is only rarely mentioned today, but the memory of it still distorts the view of St Kitts across The Narrows from Nevis.

Independence

After the new State came into being in 1967, and while not going as far as the Anguillans in rejecting rule from St Kitts, the people of Nevis displayed no great enthusiasm for the union. Their elected representatives invariably were drawn from political parties based in Nevis. In the State's parliament these functioned as the official opposition to the ruling, St Kitts-based, Labour Party. This situation lasted until 1980. In the general election held that year three members of a party called the People's Action Movement were elected to seats in St Kitts. By entering into a coalition with the two successful members of the Nevis Reformation Party they were able to oust the Labour Party from office and form a new Government. The Nevisian representatives were able to drive a very hard bargain, insisting on some sort of federal arrangement, with Nevis having considerable political autonomy. When the same coalition Government brought about full independence for the State on 19 September 1983 the constitution made specific provision for Nevis to have its own administration and legislature, consisting of an eight-seat Nevis Island Assembly led by a Premier under a Deputy Governor-General.

The Parliament of St Kitts-Nevis meets in Basseterre, where the National Assembly now consists of eight elected members from St Kitts and three from Nevis. As there is no Island Assembly for St Kitts this produces the slightly anomalous situation whereby the Nevis representatives have a say in the internal affairs of the larger island, without any reciprocal right for the representatives of St Kitts, with regard to Nevis. That this, to the outside observer, rather top-heavy and cumbersome administration of two very small islands works at all says much for the commonsense and degree of compromise shown by the leadership of both.

The forced marriage of Nevis with St Kitts in 1882 was not wanted by either partner. The events of the next century, which reached an horrific climax in the *Christena* disaster, did little to encourage either to overlook what it saw as the other's vices. It now remains to be seen whether the present arrangements will erode or increase the desire for a divorce. Meanwhile the State, under a Governor-General who represents the Queen, is a fine example of a parliamentary democracy. The ruling coalition is vigorously opposed by the rump of the Labour Party in the National Assembly, the judiciary is free of any Government interference or restrictions, and the Constitution contains safeguards of the fundamental rights and freedoms.

In the years since the Second World War the life of the majority of Kittitians has improved immeasurably. What has not changed greatly in these years, or indeed at any time during the past three hundred years, is the general appearance of the island. For the passenger in a cruise ship or the skipper of a yacht, from a few miles out to sea, St Kitts still looks much as it did to the captain of an eighteenth century slaver, or to a nineteenth century member of the 'plantocracy' coming out to inspect his property. Sugar-cane fields were to be seen all around the island then, just as they are today. The overwhelming dominance of the island's economy by a single product may have diminished somewhat in the last thirty or forty years, but still in St Kitts today nowhere – except among the dry hills of the south-eastern peninsula – is it possible to escape from some association with sugar.

| 6 |
The sugar industry

Sugar was first used as a food in Polynesia, but it was the Indians in about 8000 BC who first discovered a method of extracting the juice from cane stems. The word 'sugar' comes from the Indian *sarkara*. The Persians introduced sugar-cane to the eastern Mediterranean lands, and from there the Arabs brought sugar to Europe, where for a long time it was a luxury commodity. Columbus carried some cane to the New World on his second voyage and it was soon being grown extensively in Brazil, Mexico and Cuba. Within a century of its introduction into the New World, just to complete the story, sugar-cane had been carried across the Pacific to the Philippines and across the Indian Ocean to Indonesia. After that it was only a matter of time before it was found in Hawaii and the South Sea Islands, thus completing its journey around the world. In the eastern Caribbean cane was not grown before the 1640s. It was brought to the islands by Portuguese Jews expelled from Brazil, and by Dutch merchants who were keen to encourage the produc-

Sugar Plantation (MICHAEL BOURNE)

tion of a new crop in which they could then trade. Introduced first into the French islands it soon spread to all the rest. Sugar was being produced in Barbados by 1642 and the first cane was planted in St Kitts six years later.

The sugar plantations

The method of growing sugar-cane then (and it has changed very little since) involved covering a field with parallel lines of small trenches, about three feet apart and six inches deep. Into these pieces of cane were laid end to end and covered with soil. With the right amount of water, of which there was no shortage in St Kitts, every knot in the cane (which resembles bamboo) soon put out a root and a shoot. Within about fifteen months the new canes would be about eight feet high and one inch in diameter, and ready for cutting. Each cane was cut close to the ground, stripped of its top and bound into a faggot to be taken to the crushing mill. From the cut stumps new shoots would soon spring up to produce the next crop. This was called the 'ratoon', from the Spanish word for a new shoot. As many as four ratoons could be taken before the field needed to be re-ploughed. By regular planting at intervals over a period of several months it was possible to ensure that all the cane did not ripen at the same time. Throughout the period between planting and harvesting the fields had to be kept weeded. The most expensive and only sizeable piece of mechanical equipment needed on the plantation was the sugar mill. The roller mill had been invented in Europe in the fifteenth century. It consisted of three upright wooden rollers, usually sheathed in iron, on pivots. The centre one was turned by wind, running water or animals, turning the other two by means of cog-wheels. After the cane had been cut it had to be crushed within the next twenty-four hours to produce sugar of a marketable quality. As the transporting of the cane faggots from the fields was a slow business, involving carts, pack animals or just human shoulders, no more than about three hundred acres could be serviced by one mill.

The operation of even a small plantation involved a prodigious amount of unremitting and extremely hard labour. If the owner utilised his land to its maximum advantage, with cane being planted and reaped in continuous succession, the work-load rarely eased off from one year's end to the next. The slaves imported to do this

Work at the sugar factory handling the trash (BRIAN DYDE)

work, once the settlers had switched to producing sugar and needed to clear land of forest, had a life expectancy which barely reached double figures. As a ratio of about one slave to each acre was necessary to operate a plantation efficiently the turn-over was high. A constant supply of fresh slaves was a prime requirement and the *Prince of Orange* (from which many drowned themselves in 1737) was only one of many hundreds of such vessels which brought them to St Kitts between the time sugar was introduced and when the slave trade was made illegal in 1807.

After reaching its peak in the late 1700s the production of sugar declined throughout the nineteenth century, nearly ceasing altogether on several occasions in the last hundred years. The growing of sugar beet in Europe, the emancipation of the slaves, and the increase in number of countries growing sugar-cane world-wide, all contributed to depress the industry in St Kitts and to threaten the whole economy.

Nationalisation

The industry was saved from extinction in 1912 by the opening of a central sugar factory, capable of processing the whole of the island's crop. This replaced the individual mills and boiling-houses on the various estates. It came into operation just in time for the revival in the price of sugar brought about by the First World War. This improvement lasted little longer than the war itself, and by the beginning of the 1930s there were less than 7000 acres under cultivation. By this time the population had decreased to less than 20 000. Since the last years of the previous century, when they had numbered more than 30 000, Kittitians had emigrated steadily, finding work and new lives in the USA, Cuba, the Dominican Republic and Panama, as well as in some of the neighbouring islands.

The 1935 disturbances could well have signalled the end of the industry once again, but it was saved by the outbreak of another world war. Throughout the Second World War, and until 1952, the entire sugar output of St Kitts was bought by the United Kingdom at a guaranteed price. In the year this agreement ended a record 51 000 tons was produced, from some 16 000 acres spread over sixty estates. As the labour force was then about 8000 strong, it can be seen that although the number of workers required to produce sugar efficiently had effectively been halved since the days of slavery, the operation of the estates still needed a considerable amount of manual labour.

The ending of the UK purchasing agreement plunged the industry into recession, and this grew steadily worse for the next two decades. In 1973 public money was put into the 'Sugar Rescue Operation', and three years later the State acquired the central sugar factory. At the same time an attempt was made by the Government to nationalise the sugar estates. Because of the way this was handled the estate owners took the matter to court and nationalisation was declared to be unconstitutional. The matter was not resolved for many years. Nationalisation proceeded in defiance of the court's ruling, and the dispossessed owners had to wait a long time before receiving any compensation.

Today about ninety per cent of all arable land is publicly owned, with that which is used for growing sugar-cane being divided into just over thirty estates. The sugar they produce, around 30 000 tons a year, is produced at a loss, even though it is sold to both the EEC and the USA at preferential prices. None is sold to other Caribbean

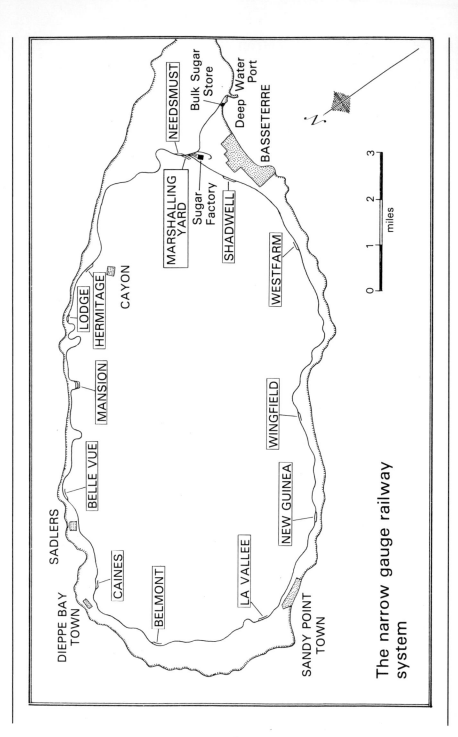

The narrow gauge railway system

**Locomotive number 8 – the first railway engine
in use on St Kitts** (BRIAN DYDE)

countries because to do so would involve selling at the true market price – thus making the losses in production that much greater.

The railway

Regardless of how the fortunes of the industry have fluctuated over the years, the sugar factory has remained working throughout. During 'crop time', now as in every year since it opened, an enormous quantity of cane is needed each day to make its operation worthwhile. The light railway which delivers cane has a history slightly longer than that of the factory itself. The first stretch of line was laid between a pier at the eastern end of Basseterre Bay and a site about one mile to the north, and from 1910 to 1912 the first locomotive shuttled up and down this line, hauling materials and the equipment used to construct the factory. This locomotive

**A compound girder bridge at Wingfield Road
(overleaf)** (BRIAN DYDE)

(number 8 as it was called subsequently) is still in existence although taken out of service long ago. As seems to be the case with the railway system of any country, in which old locomotives are seldom broken up but rather allowed to rust away in some disused siding, number 8 can be found in the sugar factory's railway 'graveyard'. In spite of the rust and one or two missing parts it is still in very fair condition. While the modern interest in industrial archaeology may not yet be apparent in St Kitts, when it is number 8 will make an excellent exhibit in a future industrial museum.

As the factory was being constructed the railway was extended from it. The 'west feeder line' was laid from the factory's marshalling yard as far as Palmetto Point, about four miles from Basseterre, and in the opposite direction the 'north-east feeder line' ran for about seven miles to Nicola Town. It was not until 1925 that the system was extended around the northern part of the island to make the circular single-line track which remains in existence today. The thirty-inch gauge permanent way is made of thirty pound rail sections secured to two-inch steel trough sleepers about two feet apart. As no ballast was used and the sleepers are laid directly on to the road-bed this causes some problems in maintaining a clear track, particularly during and after heavy rainstorms. The average gradient of the permanent way is no more than one per cent, with curves no greater than three degrees except in the marshalling yard. The line around the island, together with the spur leading to the Bulk Sugar Storage near the original 'factory pier', is about thirty miles long. There are probably another ten miles of track associated with the sidings and the marshalling yard. Because of the deep 'guts', the normally dry river beds which break up the narrow coastal plain, the laying of the line involved the building of a large number of bridges. There are twenty-six in all, the longest being the 360-foot six span compound girder bridge over Lodge Gut near Nicola Town on the north coast. As the bridges are hardly wider than the permanent way, and the highest is some 75 feet above the ground, the engine driver looking out of the window of a cab which is five or six feet wide needs to have a head for heights.

The rolling stock, which was all made in Great Britain, consists of nineteen locomotives, over seven hundred cane wagons, and about another hundred assorted wagons for carrying sugar, molasses, bagasse and maintenance crews. The locomotives are all 0-6-0 diesel engines – Hunslets, Rustons and Whitcombs, with one Armstrong

'Churchill', the A Davenport 145 hp railway engine – the only one with a name (BRIAN DYDE)

and one Davenport. They range in size from 40 hp Rustons used for yard shunting to the 150 hp Hunslet which is the largest of the mainline haulage locomotives. They are all known by their numbers except for the 145 hp Davenport; this engine, which as number 13 was involved in more than its fair share of accidents and derailments, was given the name *Churchill* in order to get rid of the unlucky number. Each train hauling sugar-cane is made up of the locomotive, a brake tender, and up to twenty-seven wagons. The crew of three consists of the driver and two switchmen.

The rail system is divided into four sections. One train operates a shuttle service with cane wagons at the northern end of the island, carrying cane from the northern estates to the sidings near Belle View on the north coast and near Sandy Point on the west coast. From Belle View, the other trains work the Cayon or North line, while others work the West line from Sandy Point, both terminating at the factory. Another shuttle service operates from the factory, with a train which carries raw sugar to the Bulk Storage facility, close to the deep water port. Within the three main sections there are twelve transfer sidings with loading and passing loops. Cane is brought to these from the various estates in large carts, towed by tractors. Each tractor tows two carts, each one carrying one and a half tons. The cane is stock-piled at the siding and loaded mechanically into the railway wagons, each of which can hold three tons. As the factory is capable of handling over 2700 tons, or 900 wagon-loads, of cane a day it will be seen that the operation of the railway is no simple matter. In the middle of the 'crop season', which lasts from February to July, trains are running constantly from very early in the morning until late into the night.

The transfer sidings are roughly two and a half miles apart all around the island. The railway is operated on a block running system, with all the trains and every siding in VHF radio communication with the central traffic control office at the marshalling yard. Clearance for a train to enter the 'block' between any two sidings is given by the traffic controller working through the signalman at each siding. The controller maintains an unsophisticated but nonetheless effective visual display board, with incoming and outgoing trains indicated by pegs in the appropriate blocks. While the system is not perfect, and the occasional collision, derailment or accident has been known to happen, there has been no major calamity connected with the railway throughout its history.

No one travelling around the island, even when the crop is not being reaped, can fail to be aware of the railway's existence – the road and the railway track cross repeatedly and level-crossings are everywhere. During 'crop time', and especially for the railway enthusiast, the clatter of train wheels, the red warning flags fluttering at the crossings, and the sound of the locomotive whistles, add even more interest to a tour of the island. While the future of sugar may be uncertain the railway will retain its importance to the end; it is even possible to envisage a modern version of locomotive number 8 shuttling parts of a dismantled factory back to the port for sale as scrap overseas. What is more certain is that a St Kitts without its quaint, rattling, busy little railway will be a rather less interesting and individual island.

The future of sugar

When St Kitts became an 'Associated State' in 1967 a new State flag was introduced. This was a simple design with three vertical panels in different colours, with a sugar-cane plant represented in the centre panel. Sixteen years later when the island became fully independent it was thought necessary to change the flag once again. The present national flag is multi-coloured, representing sunshine and the fertility of the island, as well as abstract themes such as 'the struggle from slavery', 'African heritage', 'hope' and 'liberty', with no reference to sugar or sugar-cane.

Among the eighty or more countries which grow sugar-cane St Kitts ranks in the last fifteen, the island's annual output of sugar amounting to much less than one per cent of the total world production figure. If the island stopped producing raw sugar altogether it is hardly likely that anyone in the rest of the world would notice. But, with nearly half the work-force still in the industry, such a move is out of the question. For some time yet a large number of Kittitians are going to remain tied to the cane fields in much the same way as their forefathers were. Their consolation will be that their wages, working conditions and above all their expectations – unlike those of their predecessors – can only continue to improve. The outlook is brightened by the present administration's efforts at creating a more diversified economy. An increasing amount of land is being put to other uses, whether to produce cash crops, or to accommodate small factories, light industrial concerns and tourist facilities.

These measures, following on from similar ones introduced over the last two decades or so, have had their effect. However unchanging the appearance of the island may be from offshore, the face of St Kitts *has* been altered in recent years. This is especially so in the central part around Basseterre. For the majority of the population the quality of life is quite different and appreciably better than it was even one or two generations ago. Not surprisingly, when looking at some of the things which have helped to bring about this change, it will be seen that they have very little to do with the sugar industry.

| 7 |
A changing economy

Of all the physical developments which have taken place in the island, and helped to bring about changes to the way of life in recent years, probably the two most important were the construction of a port capable of berthing deep-draught ships, and the enlarging of the airport to enable it to handle international flights.

The deep water port

Basseterre Bay has always been the main anchorage, but although it is on the lee side of the island it has its limitations as a safe and sheltered harbour. It is exposed to the south-easterly winds which blow from time to time, and any sea swell from the south (a not infrequent occurrence) makes it an uncomfortable and sometimes

The deep water port, Basseterre (MICHAEL BOURNE)

dangerous place to anchor a ship. Until the beginning of the 1980s only vessels such as inter-island schooners, the Nevis ferry and the occasional small freighter could berth alongside, using the Customs pier in the middle of Basseterre waterfront. All ships of any size had to anchor off and all freight had to be lightered to and from the shore. This all changed in 1981 when a proper port, with berths for deep-draught ships, was built at the eastern end of the bay. This transformed the harbour. The scene of a bulk sugar freighter moored in the middle of the bay, loading huge sacks of raw sugar from lighters bumping against its sides, and familiar to generations of Kittitians, vanished for ever. All cargo operations now take place at the port, including the loading of sugar. Having been brought to the Bulk Storage by rail it is transported the final few hundred yards to the dockside in bins towed by tractors. From these it is transferred into the ship's holds by a mechanical loading device. The old lighters have long since disappeared and the only vessels which are now seen along the Basseterre waterfront are a few fishing boats and one or two pleasure craft, with only the Nevis ferry making regular use of the Customs pier.

The new port has also made St Kitts more attractive to the operators of the many passenger ships which cruise the Caribbean. The number of cruise ship visitors has risen from around 7000 before the port opened to well over 50 000 each year. These short-term visitors are made just as welcome as any others, but it is those who stay for longer periods who have made the greater impact on the island. That such tourists now arrive in, for St Kitts, large numbers is due to the ease with which the island can be reached by air, and to the fact that the airport is capable of handling international flights.

Golden Rock Airport

In 1945 an airstrip was made on a stretch of level ground at the Golden Rock estate about a mile to the north of Basseterre. The original airport, which opened two years later could be used only by small aircraft flying to and from the surrounding islands, with the main service being to Antigua, where it was necessary to go to connect with an international flight. The present 8000-foot runway was laid down in the 1970s and a new air terminal building constructed at the beginning of the 1980s. While the latter is probably one of the least attractive of such buildings anywhere in the region,

Golden Rock is a recognised international airport capable of handling all modern aircraft, with the exception of the Concorde and wide-bodied 'jumbo' aircraft with maximum payload. There are over 20 000 aircraft movements each year, of which three-quarters are scheduled flights. Direct services are maintained with the USA and Canada, as well as with all the neighbouring islands. Connections with flights to and from Europe are made in Antigua or St Martin. More than 90 000 passengers use the airport annually.

Compared with either St Martin or Antigua the tourist industry in St Kitts is very small. Only in recent years has the annual number of visitors reached five figures. The part played in the economy by this new industry is a minor one and tourism has a long way to go before it begins to rival sugar. The old Golden Rock sugar estate may long since have disappeared, engulfed by the airport, but no one arriving by air today can fail to be aware of the continuing dominance of the sugar industry. The most fertile region on the island is in the valley to the north of the airport, between Monkey Hill and the Canada Hills, and the cane fields start at the boundary fence. On the opposite side of the airport, close to the terminal building, is the sugar factory. Regardless of the fact that the topography allows no other disposition, it seems very fitting that the factory and the airport are side by side. The factory is the core of the sugar industry and represents over 350 years of the life and history of St Kitts. The airport is the hub of the tourist industry and symbolises, if not the whole, a large part of the future of the island. The sugar used by the passengers in the aircraft using Golden Rock comes in small paper envelopes – and is undoubtedly grown in some other country. St Kitts has a long way to go before its stores and supermarkets have to stock the same sort of sugar in larger containers, to the exclusion of its own, but it is left to the reader to decide which, between the factory and the airport, will outlast the other.

Agricultural diversification

Now that sugar is being produced at a loss it is inconceivable that the amount of land now growing sugar-cane will ever be increased. The likelihood of sugar estates decreasing in size has already been recognised and efforts are being made to grow other crops. The diversification programme has got little further than the establishment of a few farms growing vegetables in quantities which may or may not meet local needs. While land is available for small-holdings it can only be leased; the Government being unwilling to sell agricultural land or to encourage large-scale farming. While it is possible to understand official reluctance to allow large areas of land to slip back into private ownership, when it took the best part of three and a half centuries to wrest it out of private hands, the present policy could appear retrogressive.

In the past the cane field workers were always allowed to grow ground provisions in small patches they had cleared on the sides of the mountains above the cane fields. The creation of a class of what would be little more than peasant farmers, even though they might be working better land nearer to sea-level, in the modern day and age is not a viable proposition. This approach towards encouraging locals to grow crops other than sugar-cane to some extent conflicts with official thinking about foreign investment in agriculture. In this case the accent is on attracting overseas invest-ment in 'agro-based industries' – ranging from the 'processing' of peanuts and fruit to the manufacturing of soups, salad oils and coir rugs – all of which would require large acreages of land being given over to intensive cultivation. However, in spite of this apparent disagreement over just how the agricultural sector of the economy should be developed, it is understood by all Kittitians that changes must take place. Sugar has dominated life for so long that it is under-standably difficult for anyone – in or out of Government – even to imagine the island without sugar-cane, or to visualise what other crops could replace it.

Turning a cockleshell into a frigate

While the importance of sugar is declining slowly that of the newest factor in the economy is expanding rapidly. The first hotel catering exclusively for tourists was built in the 1950s on the beach of Cockleshell Bay, looking directly across The Narrows towards Nevis. Throughout its existence it was accessible only by boat from Basseterre. Although, in offering privacy above everything else, it was not typical of the tourist accommodation which came later, it can be seen as having been built at least a generation too early. At the end of 1989, after two years of construction, the first road to the south-eastern tip of the island was completed. Its six-mile length

Frigate Bay Resort (MICHAEL BOURNE)

not only opened up all of the peninsula, including Cockleshell Bay, for development but for the first time gave Kittitians the opportunity of visiting a part of their homeland most of them had never set foot on before. The area of the peninsula is about ten per cent of that of the whole island, with plenty of room for the siting of hotels, golf courses, yacht marinas, tennis courts, jetties and water sports centres, as well as providing scope for private residential developments. The first resort construction was scheduled to start at the end of 1990. Fortunately, before any such building project was agreed, or the road even completed, a regulatory body had been established in order to control the development of the whole area and to protect the environment. The South-east Peninsula Land Development and Conservation Board is modelled on a similar body established about fifteen years earlier to oversee the development of the area at the north-west end of the new road, the Frigate Bay Resort.

Until the early 1970s the low-lying land between the Conaree Hills and Sir Timothy's Hill, and bordered by Frigate Bay in the south and North Frigate Bay on the opposite coast, was just another useless part of the south-eastern peninsula. Until then its only value had been as a source of salt and as a rough pasture for a few head of semi-wild stock. With the setting up of a Frigate Bay Development

Corporation, and the drawing up of a plan to develop an 'integrated tourist resort', the whole area was transformed into prime real estate. The road leading to the resort from Basseterre crosses a saddle in the hills. The transformation in the landscape from one side of the hills to the other is quite remarkable. On one side the cane fields, which probably have been there since the days of Saint-Christophe and represent all that is traditional in St Kitts, and on the other a manicured golf course surrounded by hotels, condominium blocks, restaurants, beach apartments and private houses, with their pillars, porticoes, sun awnings and swimming pools reflecting all that is new on the island.

At the centre of the resort is the island's largest hotel, previously the Royal St Kitts, now part of Jack Tar Village. Around it along North Frigate Bay, and overlooking Frigate Bay, is more tourist accommodation. Private houses have been built on the eastern slopes of the Conaree Hills, mostly by non-nationals as holiday homes. A large part of the resort is intended to be occupied by private dwellings and property here 'may be purchased and sold by non-residents without formality'.

The start of the Frigate Bay project inspired developments elsewhere. By the time the original Royal St Kitts hotel opened in 1976 there were already another five hotels catering mainly for tourists in other parts of the island. There was also an increase in the number of guest-houses being opened and beach apartments being built. Conaree beach, to the north of Frigate Bay resort, suddenly became a much more valuable stretch of land. Its villas and cottages, many for rental to tourists, now almost join up with the buildings lining North Frigate Bay. Today there is a complete range of tourist accommodation, including several very attractive 'inns' in former estate 'great houses',

The entry formalities for tourists are straightforward. No visa is needed for nationals of the United Kingdom, British Commonwealth and EEC countries, the USA and certain South American countries. The visitor is required to give an accommodation address before being allowed entry. As there is no tourist or accommodation bureau at the airport arrival without having previously arranged accommodation will cause both the prospective visitor and the immigration officer some heartache. Information about the accommodation available and the island generally is obtainable from

St Kitts	St Kitts-Nevis Tourist Board
	Church Street
	PO Box 132
	Basseterre
	Tel: (809) 465 2620

Canada	St Kitts-Nevis Tourism Office
	11 Yorkville Avenue, Suite 508
	Toronto
	Ontario
	M4W 1L3
	Tel: (416) 921 7717

Great Britain	Rosamunde Bern & Associates
	15 Wardour Mews
	D'Arblay Street
	London W1V 3FF
	Tel: (071) 437 9475

USA	St Kitts-Nevis Tourist Board
	414 East 75th Street
	New York
	NY 10021
	Tel: (212) 535 1234

Tim Benford Associates
1464 Whippoorwill Way
Mountainside
New Jersey 07092
Tel: (201) 232 6701

All the hotels observe the division of the year into a 'winter' season lasting from mid-December to mid-April, and a 'summer' season which lasts for the rest of the year, when the rates are much lower. A ten per cent service charge is levied on all hotel bills, in addition to a Government tax of seven per cent.

The Ocean Terrace Inn's Fisherman's Wharf
(overleaf) (MICHAEL BOURNE)

The industrial estates programme

St Kitts is in the happy position of having a thriving, if not at present particularly profitable agricultural industry at the same time as it is becoming an increasingly attractive tourist destination (the number of such visitors arriving by air passed the 50 000 figure for the first time in 1986). That the part of the island with the most appeal for tourists is of no agricultural value is a distinct bonus. It is also gratifying that the other new factor in the economy, the establishment of an industrial sector, threatens none of the farming land, nor lessens the attraction of the island for visitors.

For at least fifty years after 1921 anyone referring to a factory in St Kitts had to be talking about the sugar factory. This was the only manufacturing plant and the only employer of a proper industrial work-force until the 1960s. Because of its unique facilities – machine shops, processing machinery, repair shops and production equipment – it acquired a status far higher than that of similar establishments in other parts of the world. With a hierarchy of managerial, technical, accounting and clerical staff, complete with apprenticeship and other training schemes, it functioned in some respects as a quasi-vocational training institute. Many of the island's present engineers, businessmen and technicians began their working lives 'in the factory', acquiring some skill or expertise which later enabled them to move on to better things. Even some of the island's leading political figures started off life there. Robert Bradshaw, who was Premier from 1967 until his death in 1978, was sacked from his job as a machinist in 1940 when he became a trade union organiser. One of his fellow workers, Paul Southwell, also became a trade unionist and later a politician.

Southwell became the island's first Chief Minister in 1960, and it was he who introduced measures which led to the sugar factory losing its singular position. As part of a plan to diversify the economy legislation was introduced to encourage investment in manufacturing, processing and assembly plants. The 'Pioneer Industries Ordinance' made provision for the usual import duty exemption and tax relief for anyone setting up a new industry and was aimed specifically at attracting foreign investors. This paid off and today there are two industrial estates, close to the airport and the harbour, with factories producing electrical goods, clothing, footwear, boats, electronic units, and furniture.

The current Fiscal Incentives Act continues to offer overseas investors tax holidays, income tax rebates, import duty concessions and unlimited repatriation of profits. Further expansion of the industrial estates is planned, and more information about the opportunities being offered can be obtained from

Ministry of Trade & Industry
PO Box 186
Basseterre
St Kitts
Tel: (809) 465 2302

The industrial estates programme could not have been contemplated, and the tourist industry would have been stillborn, if the island had remained without an airport capable of handling international flights or a port suitable for use by deep-draught shipping. That both of these sectors of the economy flourish today is due not only to the presence of these two facilities, but also to the factories and the main tourist resort being located close to the main source of labour. While the agricultural workers still live in the various villages around the main part of the island the bulk of the rest of the work-force lives in or near Basseterre – with the factory estates on the doorstep and Frigate Bay less than three miles away.

| 8 |
Basseterre – then and now

Early days

The town of Basseterre was founded by d'Esnambuc in 1625 but probably did not amount to very much for the first twenty years or so. De Poincy took over in 1639 and ruled Saint-Christophe for the next twenty-one years. Through his efforts the settlement on the edge of Basseterre Bay took on the appearance of a proper town. So much so that, within a few years of de Poincy's death in 1660, a contemporary writer was able to describe it as:

A Town of good bigness, whose Houses are well built, of Brick, Freestone and Timber: where the Merchants have their Storehouses; and is well inhabited by Tradesmen, and are well served with such Commodities, both for the Back, and Belly, together with Utensils for the Houses, and Plantations, as they have occasion of, in exchange for such Commodities, which are the product of the Island. Here is a fair, and large Church, as also a publique-Hall, for the administration of Justice;

Independence Square, Basseterre (MICHAEL BOURNE)

*Here is also a very fair Hospital. Here is also a stately Castle,
being the Residence of the Governor, most pleasantly seated,
at the foot a a high Mountain, not far from the Sea, having
spacious Courts, delightful Walks, and Gardens, and enjoyeth
a curious prospect.*

The building of the 'stately Castle' (which in fact was about three
miles away from the town) was very much in keeping with de
Poincy's autocratic rule. A description of the building and what
remains of it today is given elsewhere. Like many of the buildings
in the town it suffered much damage from a severe earthquake in
1689, but because of its remote situation it was spared further
damage during the various Anglo-French conflicts of the seventeenth
century. Basseterre suffered greatly during these wars and by the
time the British took possession of the whole island after 1713
probably there were not too many of the original buildings still
standing. It took a number of years after the Treaty of Utrecht to
sort out the problems of land ownership in what had been Saint
Christophe, and the seat of administration was not transferred from
Old Road until 1727. Since then Basseterre has been the capital and
the commercial centre of the whole island.

Historic sites and buildings

The town today, despite its French name, is very much a British
colonial creation. Because of the destruction brought about by two
hurricanes, earthquakes, fires and floods during the last two and
a half centuries, nothing now remains of the original French town.
The oldest buildings are probably some of those around what is now
called **Independence Square**. The central gardens and surrounding
streets were laid out on land purchased in 1750, so any of the
original buildings must date from after this time. For a long time
the centre of the political, commercial and social life of the town,
it was known until 1983 by the more cultured and attractive name
of Pall Mall Square. A year before this change took place, and adding
to the list of disasters which have beset the town, one of the oldest
buildings in the Square, housing the court and the public library,
was destroyed by fire. The present-day centre of the town is a little
to the west in **The Circus**, a wide circular road junction which was
created after the 'Great Fire' of 1867. The ornate tower in the centre

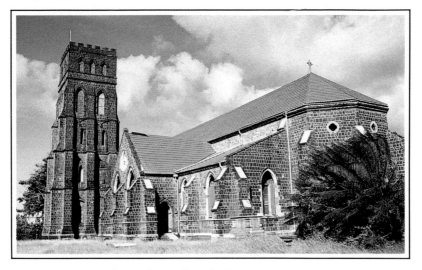

St George's Anglican Church, Basseterre (MICHAEL BOURNE)

is the **Berkeley Memorial Clock Tower and Drinking Fountain**, erected in honour of some long-forgotten legislator and estate owner of the last century.

The Honourable Thomas Berkeley Hardtman Berkeley is not the only bigwig of days gone by whose name is still connected with the town, but whose existence is otherwise totally forgotten. Soon after the British acquisition of the town several forts were built to protect the seaward approaches. The one on the headland at the western end of the bay was named **Fort Thomas**, after Sir George Thomas who was Governor of the Leeward Islands in the middle of the eighteenth century. It was built on the site of a French fort which dated from the earliest days of the settlement. On the opposite side of the bay the present port occupies the site of **Fort Smith**, of which little is known and nothing remains. Fort Street, in the middle of the town, is the only reminder of a third fort, which used to stand in the centre of the waterfront. Yet another fort was built in the early nineteenth century out of sight of the town on Frigate Bay. Nothing very much is known about any of them; they never

The Berkeley Memorial clock in the centre of The Circus, Basseterre (opposite) (MICHAEL BOURNE)

The Presbytery next door to the Roman Catholic Co-cathedral (BRIAN DYDE)

saw much action and it is unlikely that any of them amounted to very much. Today the only real remains are those of Fort Thomas in the grounds of the hotel of the same name. Apart from this fort and some of the buildings around Independence Square, there is not much in the town pre-dating the nineteenth century.

Basseterre is essentially a Victorian town with some twentieth century, and invariably ugly, accretions. Much of its charm comes from a general 'old-fashioned' appearance, which can be appreciated in the wood and stonework, the decoration of the private houses, and in the architecture of some of the older public buildings. The official residence of the Governor-General, to the north-west of the town centre, is a good example of British tropical colonial architecture. It was built as a rectory, but has been used as **Government House** since 1882. Although not open to the public it can be viewed from several aspects from the surrounding roads. The large church more or less in the centre of the town is another example of the British architectural tradition, although in this case neither tropical nor colonial. In fact, **St George's Anglican Church**, with its black stonework, is more reminiscent of a parish church in some industrial town in the north of England. It is saved from any further such invidious comparison by its large and well-kept churchyard with its splendid trees, lawns and tropical shrubs. It dates from 1869, when it was built to replace the previous church lost in the 'Great Fire' two years earlier. The handsome, four-square **Methodist Church** just to the north is slightly older, having been erected in 1825 and extensively restored a century later. The other major church is the **Co-cathedral of the Immaculate Conception** on the eastern side of Independence Square. While this dates only from 1928 it was built on very traditional lines which fit nicely into the town's Victorian image. The Presbytery next door is probably the most attractive building in Basseterre.

The **Treasury Building** in the centre of the waterfront was designed with an archway situated in such a position as to form an entry portal to the town for passengers landing on the pier directly in front of it. From the time it was built at the end of the nineteenth century, until the end of the Second World War, it housed almost the entire administration of the island. Although only two storeys in height, and regardless of the fact that the Treasury pier has been allowed to fall into such a state of disrepair that little now remains above the surface of the sea, the Treasury remains an imposing

The Treasury Building on the waterfront (MICHAEL BOURNE)

building. If it has long since lost its function of providing a gateway to the island it is still the one building which other West Indians most identify with Basseterre. When painted up for a State occasion it adds visibly to what is otherwise a rather humdrum waterfront.

The Nevis ferry

The Treasury pier used to be one of three, side by side, in the middle of the waterfront. Today only the central one, the **Customs pier**, remains standing and in daily use. Its main role now that all cargo work takes place at the deep water port is to act as the terminal for the ferry which operates between St Kitts and Nevis. This service continued to experience more than its fair share of bad luck even after the *Christena* disaster. The ferry which replaced that wretched boat was subsequently driven ashore by a passing hurricane, refloated, but then wrecked once more a couple of years later. After rusting away on the beach between the Treasury and Customs piers for a few more years it was eventually towed away and sunk in deep water. The present ferry came into service in the early 1980s.

However, the *Caribe Queen* is not only a different type of vessel – having been built for fast passenger-carrying operations in the Gulf of Mexico oilfields – but is operated in a different way from in the past. It is now very much the *Nevis* ferry, providing a service for the people of that island. The *Caribe Queen* is based at Nevis and remains at the Charlestown jetty overnight. It makes two round trips every day except on Thursdays and Sundays. The crossing takes about 45 minutes and a maximum of 150 passengers can be carried.

Island transport

Not everyone will appreciate the number of taxis which now try to park around The Circus, but at least such vehicles – in good condition and with friendly and courteous drivers – are readily available at all times of the day and for most of the night. There is a standard list of fixed fares for all trips and tours. The public bus service is run on a very casual basis, with no fixed schedules, few routes and a variety of vehicles of varying degrees of comfort. While it is possible to see most of the island using public transport of one sort or another, this is something recommended only for visitors with unlimited time, and extremely tight budget, or possessed of a masochistic desire to 'do things the hard way'.

Rental cars, as well as 'mini-mokes', motor-scooters and bicycles, are in plentiful supply. For anything but a bicycle a visitor's driving licence is needed. This costs EC$ 30 and can be obtained either at the airport of from the central police station in Basseterre. During the sugar-cane harvest the visiting driver should be wary of the many level-crossing, and be prepared to give way to the tractor-towed cane carts which feed the various sidings.

Coping with changes

Basseterre has a total area of about one square mile, but as it stretches along virtually the whole length of the bay, and parts extend inland as far as the airport runway, it appears larger than it is. Nearly half of the entire population of the island lives in the town, as has been the case for the last 150 years – now perhaps 15 000 people out of about 35 000. The slums which had been created by the influx of people from the countryside during the nineteenth century were cleared away slowly during the first half of the next century, disappearing by the 1950s. New housing estates, suitable for all income brackets, have come into being on all sides of the original town. These suburbs, from Fortlands in the west, through Greenlands, Shadwell and New Pond Site, to New Town in the east, provide better examples of town planning, sensible development, and the use of local architectural concepts and building materials than in many of the capitals of neighbouring islands. The industrial estates close to the eastern limits of the town do not intrude into the residential areas; their various factories produce little or no pollution of any sort, and for the most part are set in landscaped gardens.

The tourist industry has had its effect as well, but Basseterre is not yet the type of 'tourist Mecca' beloved of travel writers, package holiday organisers and cruise ship operators – a place filled with exotic eating places, local handicraft shops, duty-free stores, and all the superficiality which usually goes with a large transient population.

| 9 |
Basseterre – getting around

Eating and drinking

The majority of eating places depend on local patronage and serve local food, but offer visitors good value for money, with the chance to enjoy something different and the opportunity of meeting Kittitians on their home ground. To cater for those for whom a little of the local delicacy such as curried conch goes a long way, Basseterre also provides more conventional fare. A French restaurant, a pâtisserie and coffee house, and a 'gourmet restaurant' in a restored Georgian mansion, are undoubtedly only the precursors of the many other 'international', 'formal' and specialist eating places which will enlarge the choice for the hungry visitor of the future.

When it comes to drink, rum is probably the spirit which most visitors associate with the West Indies. Many varieties are available,

The Georgian House Restaurant on Independence Square
(BRIAN DYDE)

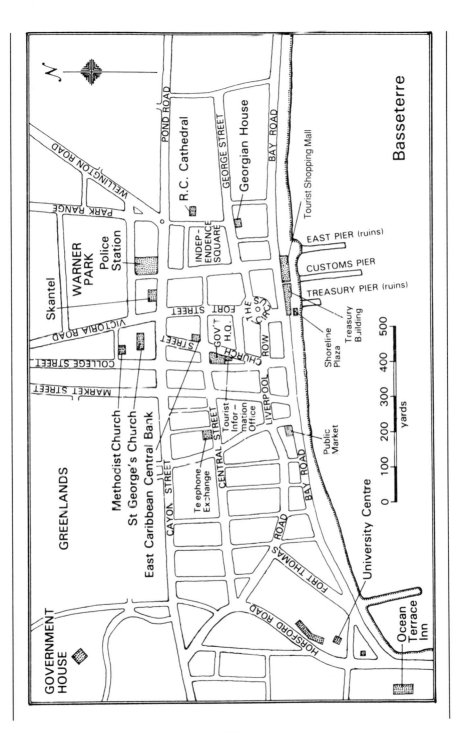

Basseterre

GOVERNMENT HOUSE

GREENLANDS

WELLINGTON ROAD

PARK RANGE

POND ROAD

R.C. Cathedral

GEORGE STREET

Georgian House

BAY ROAD

Tourist Shopping Mall

INDEP-
ENDENCE
SQUARE

EAST PIER (ruins)

CUSTOMS PIER

TREASURY PIER (ruins)

Skantel

WARNER
PARK

Police
Station

VICTORIA ROAD

FORT STREET

THE
CIRCUS

Treasury
Building

ROW

Shoreline
Plaza

GOV'T
H.Q.

CHURCH STREET

COLLEGE STREET

MARKET STREET

Methodist Church
St George's Church
East Caribbean Central Bank

LIVERPOOL
STREET

CENTRAL STREET

Tourist
Infor-
mation
Office

Te ephone
Exchange

CAYON STREET

BAY ROAD

Public
Market

0   100   200   300   400   500

yards

University Centre

FORT THOMAS ROAD

HORSFORD ROAD

Ocean
Terrace
Inn

81

any one of which will form the base of numerous highly colourful and even more highly intoxicating drinks. Regardless of the contents of the unlabelled bottle which may appear from time to time in some wayside tavern, St Kitts does not produce its own brand of rum. This may change in the future as rum distilling is among the 'agro-based industries' in which the Government is promoting investment. For those who prefer drinking beer, the island does produce its own brand. 'Carib' lager has a reputation for being one of the better beers bottled in the region: in comparison with any imported from Europe or North America it certainly will be found to be much cheaper.

Shops and shopping

Tourism has also started to have its effect on the type and quality of merchandise to be found in the town. In an official guide published in the early 1970s, shopping was dismissed in one sentence – '. . . perfumes and toilet preparations, Swiss watches, English silver, Wedgwood jasper ware and porcelain are available in small quantities in stores in Basseterre' – the accent presumably being on the word 'small'. During the intervening years not only have new stores and enterprises opened to deal specifically in the sort of articles which appeal to tourists, but these have encouraged many other shops dealing in the main with a local clientele to spruce themselves up and to extend their stock. Central Basseterre today is outwardly not much different from ten, twenty or thirty years ago. The major stores, businesses and commercial houses remain in the same place and in the same hands, but the quality of their goods and services has improved out of all recognition. The shopper will still find watches, silver, perfume and porcelain, but now at duty-free prices, and joined by many other items – cameras, silk-screened fabrics, sea island cotton batik, and well-made handicrafts. Most of the shops selling these things are obvious, with eye-catching signs and displays, but part of the pleasure in shopping in Basseterre is finding a good bargain, a handsome gift or a well-crafted souvenir in one of the smaller stores which have retained their old-fashioned and non-air-conditioned ways of doing business.

In common with the stores in the capitals of all the other Caribbean islands which were (and in a couple of cases still are) British colonies, those in Basseterre are open for business during hours which were fixed many years ago. That civilised and sensible

82

Older houses typical of the architecture of Basseterre
(MICHAEL BOURNE)

institution the siesta, which is observed in nearly every tropical and
semi-tropical town between Acapulco and Zamboanga, is unknown
here. It was never acceptable to the dour Scottish merchants and
staid British shopkeepers who dominated business life in these
islands during the nineteenth century: giving in to the climate was
not to be considered, and taking a rest from earning money in the
hottest part of the day was an alien concept in which only idle
'foreigners' indulged. As a result the usual opening hours for the
stores and businesses of Basseterre today are from 8.00 am until
noon, and from 1.00 pm to 4.00 pm daily. Those shoppers emulating
Mr Noel Coward's well-known Englishman and his deranged canine
counterpart will find an air of lethargy hanging heavily over the
streets in the afternoon, and the stores somewhat less than busy.
Except, that is, on Thursdays when, still conforming to another
peculiarly British ritual imported in colonial days, the shops do not
open in the afternoon at all.

This is of no more than passing interest. While most of the old
'British West Indies' are now independent States – and each has a
vocal minority of its populace constantly carping about neo-
colonialism – their new rulers by and large have retained all the
manners and customs of their former colonial masters. Business

hours make but one small example. The re-ordering of business life to take the climate into account, and not to continue aping the practices of London, Liverpool and Aberdeen, would be a radical step – but it is one long overdue. The Caribbean after all is very much part of *Latin* America.

Currency and banking

The hotels in St Kitts, like those in all other West Indian islands, quote their rates in US dollars. Whereas in the capitals of the more tourist-oriented islands the unwary visitor might be led to assume that all prices were quoted in the same currency, this is not the case here. For the most part prices in shops are quoted in the local currency. This is the Eastern Caribbean (EC) dollar, which is also used in Anguilla, Montserrat, Antigua & Barbuda, Dominica, St Lucia, St Vincent and Grenada. It is tied to the US dollar at the rate of

Central Street, Basseterre (BRIAN DYDE)

EC$2.70 to US$1.00. The currency is issued by the Eastern Caribbean Central Bank, which has its headquarters in Basseterre. Notes are issued to the value of 100, 20, 10, 5 dollars; there is also a one dollar note, a one dollar coin, and coins worth 50, 25, 10, 5, 2 cents and one cent.

There is no restriction on the importing or exporting of foreign currency, and exchange facilities exist at all the local banks. Credit cards and travellers cheques are accepted by most hotels and the major stores dealing with tourists. Banking hours are from 8.00 am to 1.00 pm from Monday to Thursday. On Fridays they open half an hour later and re-open in the afternoon for two hours from 3.00 pm.

Public holidays

Just as the island continues to follow British practices when it comes to business hours, so its calendar of public holidays is patterned very much on that observed in Great Britain. Stores, banks, businesses and Government offices are closed on the following days of the year:

New Year's Day
Good Friday
Easter Monday
Labour Day (first Monday in May)
Whit Monday
The Queen's Official Birthday (second Saturday in June)
August Monday (first Monday in August)
Independence Day (19 September)
Christmas Day
Boxing Day (26 December)
Carnival Day (varies from year to year)

Post Office and postage stamps

The Post Office, between the Treasury and the tourist shopping mall on the waterfront, is open during hours which do not coincide with either those of the normal business day or those or other government offices. It opens at 8.00 am but closes at 3.00 pm, except on Thursdays when it closes at 11.00 am. To meet the demands of stamp collectors a separate Philatelic Bureau was set up in 1980. This has since been relocated and is now part of the Post Office.

85

Although they form a unitary State, both St Kitts and Nevis issue their own stamps. St Kitts started doing so when the Bureau was first opened, and since then there have been four or five commemorative and a single souvenir issue each year. In addition there have been a number of other 'special' issues concerning events judged to be of 'true international importance'. While these are all probably too many to please the dedicated philatelist, to the average collector they appear very colourful and interesting. They also serve to provide the island with some excellent publicity as well as a source of revenue.

Nightlife and Carnival

For the visitor who wants more excitement in the evening than perhaps can be found from studying postage stamps (despite the fascination that 'gutter-pairs', 'imprint blocks' and 'traffic-light blocks' hold for the *cognoscenti*), St Kitts has other things to offer – but not as many as on the more 'touristy' islands. The larger hotels provide local bands and artistes, and there is a casino at Jack Tar Village at Frigate Bay. Other than this there are one or two discos in or around Basseterre which will appeal to the more youthful visitors. For anyone hoping for or requiring a sophisticated nightlife as part of a vacation, St Kitts is not the place to choose for a visit.

The sum and substance of the cultural life of the island will best be appreciated by visitors to the island during the Christmas season. The carnival which takes place in Basseterre features steel bands, brass bands, calypso singing, beauty queen contests, and talent shows. It lasts from 26 December to 2 January.

The modern festivities derive from what, in days gone by, were known as 'Christmas sports'. These were street entertainments by string bands, clowns, groups of people in fancy dress, 'moko-jumbies' (men on stilts), and 'masqueraders'. These last were bands of a dozen or more people, wearing outlandish traditional costumes, who performed exotic – and often erotic – dances as they roamed the streets. The 'sports' were a feature of the Christmas season from the plantation days onwards, but they declined in popularity after the Second World War – affected as much by the emergence of trade

The Royal St Kitts Casino at Jack Tar Village (opposite) (CHRIS HUXLEY)

Steel Band entertaining at the Ocean Terrace Inn (G W LENNOX)

unions and political parties (which wanted the workers to concentrate on forgetting the past) as by the steady increase in the numbers of people who found them too vulgar. The present-day Carnival, which dates back only to the late 1960s, retains some of the less indelicate 'sports' but is really a small replica of the Trinidad pre-Lenten Carnival. Where it differs from similar events staged in islands like Antigua is that it was never intended to be a tourist attraction. It remains very much a local festive occasion in which Kittitians can mix freely, enjoy themselves hugely, and eat, drink, dance and celebrate – if not to excess, at least to a 'good sufficiency'. By now of course it has, willy-nilly, become a tourist attraction, and the biggest and the most colourful that Basseterre has to offer – even if it lasts for only one week of the year.

Not all of the dances and parties held at this time are open to the public, but there will be plenty of entertainment and activity by both day and night in which visitors can participate. But whether they are taking part or merely looking on they will see something of the island and its people which is not apparent at any other time of the year. Fortunately, during the rest of the year St Kitts has plenty of other attractions, natural and man-made which do not last for just one week.

| 10 |

From Basseterre to Brimstone Hill

The 'tourist circuit'

To the vacationing visitor St Kitts is just a small island, divided to all outward appearance into two parts – the roughly oval-shaped mountainous area, and the long, hilly peninsula. He is likely to see the former as the 'working' part, and the latter as a typical Caribbean vacationer's playground. However, the attractions of the island are not confined to any one part any more than the tourist accommodation is all to be found at the Frigate Bay resort. The majority of them can be reached easily, as they are near the coast and close to the road which runs around the whole of the main part of the island. The remaining attractions are not so easily accessible and will appeal in the main to those who want to add something a little more adventurous or exacting to the conventional Caribbean vacation.

For most visitors, and especially those who arrive by cruise ship and remain for a matter of hours only, the standard circular tour will provide all that they ever see of the bulk of the island. While it is convenient here to describe the various sites and sights by following the route of such a tour, it is hoped that what has been read so far about St Kitts and the Kittitians will encourage the prospective sightseer not to view the attractions in isolation. These are spread out around the island with, at strategic intervals, a former estate house now turned into an alluring 'inn'. Because of this it is very tempting for the stranger, perhaps driving on the left-hand side of the road for the first time, unaccustomed to the Kittitian village dialect, and not too sure of the way in any case, to stick rigidly to the prescribed route and to pause for refreshment only where she sees that an American Express card is welcome. This is perfectly acceptable but it will provide only a very superficial glimpse of the island.

The circular tour affords an excellent opportunity to see something of the village life and to meet people who normally have no connection with tourists or tourism. The menu in the 'Silver Dollar

89

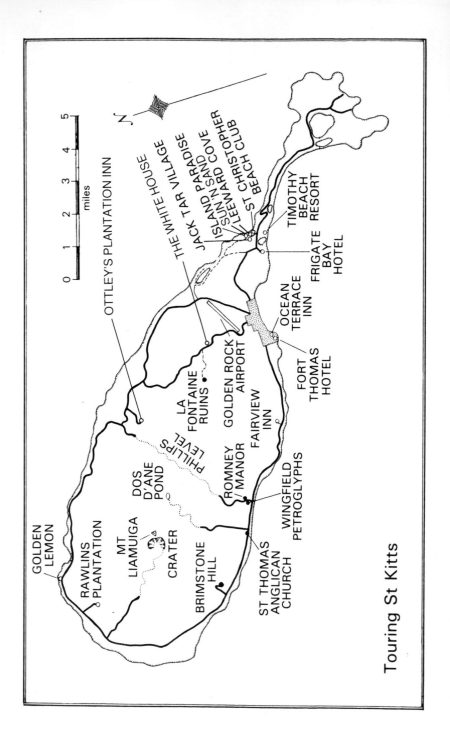

Touring St Kitts

Bar and Snackette' in ------ Village may not match that of the 'Green Lime Plantation Inn' at ------ Estate, but then neither will the prices. The roads, except during the early morning and late afternoon hours when people are going to and from Basseterre, are very quiet; anyone coming from a North American or European city will be delighted with the normal, traffic-free driving conditions. As in all other West Indian islands where English is spoken, certain sections of the community in St Kitts use a dialect, which is hard for the uninitiated to understand. As this is dropped when talking to strangers, and as Kittitians are just as friendly as any other West Indians, the English-speaking visitor will have little difficulty in making contact with people in any part of the island. For those still unsure of what is involved in touring an excellent map of St Kitts is available from the Tourist Information Office in Basseterre, which shows all the hotels as well as the places of interest.

It is recommended that the island be traversed in a clockwise direction, leaving Basseterre by the road leading along the south-west coast This introduces the visitor to the various historical sites in a better chronological order. More importantly, if the tour is begun, as it usually is, in the morning, it ensures that the sun remains behind the driver as the day progresses.

Fairview Inn, a converted estate house (MICHAEL BOURNE)

Petroglyphs and manors

The **Fairview Inn**, about three miles out of Basseterre, is the first of several estate houses which have been converted in recent years to other uses. It is a few hundred yards away from the main road on the side of a hill called Ottley's Level. Like many of the other estate houses it dates back to the early 1700s, but was allowed to fall into disrepair during the nineteenth century. It was restored and converted into the core of a small hotel during the 1960s.

Another mile or so along the coast road near the village of Challengers (which has some claim to being the first of the 'free' villages established after the slaves were freed in 1834) is **Bloody Point**. This takes its name from being the place where the Carib population was massacred in 1626. Near the roadside another half a mile further on are the remains of Stone Fort, a small fortification which gave its name to the adjacent estate. The remains are negligible and overgrown – most of the building stones having long ago been carried away for use elsewhere. The fort was erected to guard the eastern approaches to Old Road Bay, when this was still the main anchorage for St Christopher in the seventeenth century. From the site there is a good view of the bay, showing very clearly its limitations as a harbour. **Old Road Town** in the middle of the bay front is no more than a small village, but even at that it is much bigger now than it was at any time in the past. Its importance in the early days stemmed entirely from the Wingfield River which discharges into the bay through the middle of the town.

A little way inland, alongside the road from Old Road to **Wingfield Manor Estate**, is a group of black boulders, with a number of primitive drawings carved into the smooth face of the largest. These **petroglyphs** indicate the importance that this location, with its never-failing source of fresh water, had for the Caribs, who are generally accepted as the people who carved them.

The estate house at Wingfield is of no particular merit, but its close neighbour – approached from Old Road – is well worth a visit. **Romney Manor** is another estate house which has been converted. In this case it has been turned into a workshop producing batik clothing and wall hangings. The finished designs are unmistakably West Indian, and to a standard well in keeping with the splendidly

Working on one of the beautiful Caribelle Batik designs at Romney Manor (opposite) (CHRIS HUXLEY)

93

maintained premises in which they are produced. The surrounding gardens are kept up to the same standard, and are worth visiting for themselves. In the middle of a lawn in front of the house is an immense saman tree, reputedly over three hundred years old. Standing in its shade some 50 or 60 feet from its trunk leaves no room to doubt its age. The workshops are open to the public daily except on Sundays.

Inland Trails

Wingfield Estate will be bypassed by most tourists, as they turn off the road leading to it and head for Romney Manor, but it is an important staging post for the more adventurous who intend to take a hike into the mountains. The less strenuous of the two main trails which start here is that which crosses the saddle between Verchild's Mountain and the South East Range. This follows the old track which in the days of the Anglo-French division of the island enabled the British to get from one side to the other without passing through French territory. The trail across **Phillips Level** is fairly straight-forward, about six miles in length, and rising no more than about 1500 feet. It descends on the north-eastern side through the villages of Philips and Molineux.

The second trail is shorter but will take longer to hike. This winds three thousand feet up Verchild's Mountain to a small lake near the summit called **Dos d'Ane Pond** (rendered colloquially as Dodan's Pond). It is about two acres in extent and no more than four feet deep, filling the bottom of an old crater. It has never been known to dry up even during the most severe drought. When full it overflows in a sheer waterfall over the rim on the south-western side. The climb is very steep in places and it should not be undertaken lightly or without a guide.

A 'much lamented gent'

A mile further on along the coast from Old Road is the parish church of St Thomas at **Middle Island**. It is approached from the road by a footpath between rows of royal palms, stretching the entire length of the churchyard. The church is famous for being the burial place of Sir Thomas Warner. His tomb, which is under a small wooden canopy just outside the church, is covered by a marble slab bearing

Sir Thomas Warner's tomb at Middle Island (MICHAEL BOURNE)

his epitaph:

AN EPITAPH VPON THE ...
NOBLE & MVCH LAMENTED GENT' SIR
THO WARNER K^T LIEVTENANT
GENERALL OF Y^E CARRIBEE
IELAND W GOVERR OF Y^E
IELAND OF S^T CHRIST^R
WHO DEPARTED THIS
LIFE ON 10 OF
MARCH 1648

First Read then weepe when thou art hereby taught
That Warner lyes interr'd here, one that bought

With losse of Noble bloud the Illustrious Name
Of A Commander Greate in Acts of Fame.
Traynd from his youth in Armes his Courage bold
Attempted braue Exploites, and Vncontrold
By fortunes fiercest frownes hee still gaue forth
Large Narratiues of Military worth
Written with his swords poynt but what is man
In the midst of his glory and who can
Secure this Life A moment since that hee
Both by Sea and Land so long kept free
At mortal stroakes at length did yeeld
Grace to Conqueringe Death the field
FINE CORONAT

The marble slab was broken at some time in the past, and the words
and letters in bold print are missing. They are reproduced here from
the full transcription of the epitaph in the long outdated, but
nonetheless useful and interesting, '*Pocket Guide to the West Indies*'
by Sir Algernon Aspinall.

During the twenty-five years he lived in St Kitts Warner played
a major part in establishing the British in the Caribbean, and as we
have seen was directly responsible for settling Antigua, Nevis and
Montserrat. Getting on for three hundred years after Warner's death,
the same Sir Algernon Aspinall – who was a noted traveller among,
and writer about, the West Indies in the earlier part of the present
century – remarked in a book published in 1927 that:

> *As the pioneer of English colonization in the West Indies,*
> *which brought such immense wealth to this country and paved*
> *the way for the industrial revolution of the eighteenth century,*
> *Warner deserves to be included among the makers of the*
> *Empire; but while there are statues of Captain Cook, John*
> *Cabot, Stamford Raffles, and Cecil Rhodes, not one has been*
> *raised in honour of the man of Suffolk who founded our oldest*
> *group of colonies.*

Although words like 'Empire' and 'colonies' are no longer quite as
respectable as they were in 1927, Aspinall's sentiments are not
without merit. That there is still no statue or other memorial in
England, where Warner's name probably is unknown to anyone but
a handful of people, is understandable. That there is no monument

96

**The village mechanic's workshop in Middle Island
Village** (BRIAN DYDE)

in St Kitts, where according to a long homily delivered by the then deputy Premier at a service held in 1973 to mark the 350th anniversary of his landing Warner's name 'will be ever-remembered and respected in the island', is less understandable.

After the celebrations held fifty years earlier to commemorate the three hundredth anniversary a public park in Basseterre was given his name, but this today seems hardly worthy of the man. However, it should not pass unremarked that 'Warner' remains a common name in the island. While genealogy has never been, for obvious reasons, a study much pursued by West Indians in the past, there is no reason why this should continue. In these days when a general interest has been aroused among many black people in tracing their ancestry and 'roots', research into Kittitian family histories may yet become a rewarding occupation. As the four hundredth anniversary of his arrival in St Kitts draws nearer, the Warner family tree may well prove to be Sir Thomas's most lasting and worthwhile memorial.

From Bloody Point onwards, while travelling north along the coast road, the summit of Mt Liamuiga – with or without its cloud cap – can be seen inland. At the same time a much lower peak, separated from the main mountain mass and closer to the coast, seems to dominate the view to an even greater extent. This is **Brimstone Hill**, which is about three miles north-west of Old Road Town. The hill has already been mentioned in earlier chapters, when the fortifications built on it played an important part in the wars of the eighteenth century. Today the Brimstone Hill fortress, which is the next historic site on the circular tour after leaving Middle Island, is the island's main tourist attraction. As such it deserves a chapter to itself.

| 11 |

The Gibraltar of the Caribbean

Formation and fortification

The smell of sulphur which gave Brimstone Hill its name can still be detected as one walks or drives along the main road near its base. On some days the odour of bad eggs is very marked and drifts for some distance downwind. This is the only indication left of the volcanic origin of the hill, which was as a plug extruded from the side of Mt Liamuiga. This took place below the sea-level then existing and large amounts of the seabed – sedimentary limestone – were raised up on its shoulders. There are deposits of limestone on all sides of the hill except in the north-east where it is joined by a saddle to the lower slopes of the mountain. Because of these deposits the hill has a geological formation found nowhere else on the island. The nearest geological counterpart is the colossal slab of limestone resting against the bottom of the extinct volcano called The Quill

The fortress at Brimstone Hill (MICHAEL BOURNE)

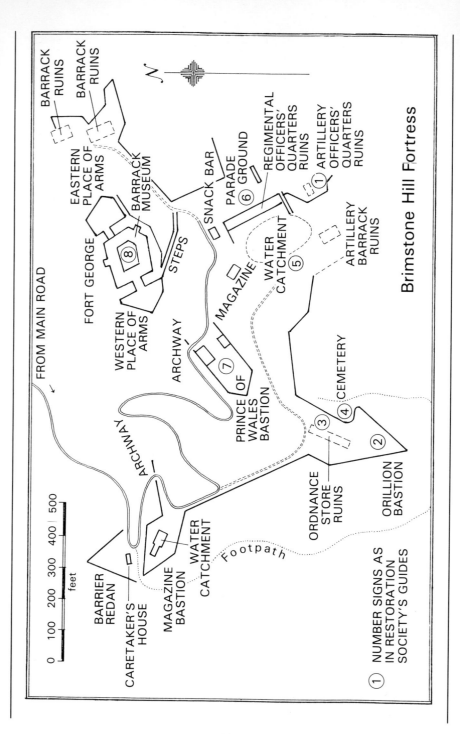

Brimstone Hill Fortress

FROM MAIN ROAD

BARRACK RUINS
BARRACK RUINS
EASTERN PLACE OF ARMS
BARRACK MUSEUM
SNACK BAR
PARADE GROUND ⑥
REGIMENTAL OFFICERS' QUARTERS RUINS
ARTILLERY OFFICERS' QUARTERS RUINS ①
FORT GEORGE
⑧
WESTERN PLACE OF ARMS
STEPS
ARCHWAY
MAGAZINE
WATER CATCHMENT
ARTILLERY BARRACK RUINS
⑤
PRINCE OF WALES BASTION
⑦
ARCHWAY
CEMETERY ④
③
② ORILLION BASTION
ORDNANCE STORE RUINS
BARRIER REDAN
CARETAKER'S HOUSE
MAGAZINE BASTION
WATER CATCHMENT
Footpath

0 100 200 300 400 500
feet

① NUMBER SIGNS AS IN RESTORATION SOCIETY'S GUIDES

100

in Sint Eustatius. This is the famous 'White Wall' which can be seen clearly from the northern end of St Kitts

The fortifications of Brimstone Hill are reached by means of a road along the northern side which doubles back on itself to climb up to the entrance at the **Barrier Redan**. At the caretaker's house, where a small entrance fee is payable, various small guides, maps and prints are on sale. The official tourist map of the island (scale 1 to 50 000) contains a plan of the whole fortress on a much larger scale. While this plan must be considered the definitive representation of all the work undertaken to defend the hill, it has its limitations as a guide to what can still be seen today. It does not differentiate between buildings and fortifications still standing, those partially ruined, and those of which nothing now remains above the ground. What it does show very adequately is how well the fortress was constructed, using the natural contours of the hill to their best advantage. The numerous bastions, barracks, offices, storerooms, magazines, workshops and other buildings of which it was comprised, were spread over thirty acres, making it one of the largest and finest works of military engineering carried out by the British in the West Indies. This work was started shortly after 1690, when the hill had been used to launch an artillery attack on a French fort near its foot, and continued in stages for the best part of the next century. The citadel on the summit and the large bastion just below it were among the last parts to be built, late in the eighteenth century. Plans to build more defence works were halted by the start of the Napoleonic Wars and then never implemented.

Dilapidation and restoration

During the long period of peace following the Congress of Vienna in 1815 the fortress continued to be manned until the early 1850s. The outbreak of the Crimean War provided the excuse the British Government must have been waiting for, and the garrison was withdrawn in 1853. As happened with the smaller forts both here and in other islands, once the troops had left and the buildings had been turned over to the local Government, decay set in very quickly. Vandalism is nothing new and has been carried out on abandoned structures since classical times. All the wooden buildings and metal fittings, including the cannon, on Brimstone Hill were soon disposed of – and a lot of the stonework followed in the years to come. Very

little is known, and with good reason, about who did this or for what purpose. One can only hope that some of the stone and brick-work was used in the homes of some of the poor cane field workers of the second half of the nineteenth century; it was after all their bonded ancestors who had hauled them up the hill in the first place.

The gradual deterioration of the fortress continued until very recent times, despite its having been recognised as a national asset and a unique historical site since the early years of this century. It is now a protected site, part of the Brimstone Hill National Park, and is administered by a keen and active Restoration Society. Since the mid-1960s a great deal of work has been carried out, both on restoring some of the buildings and in developing it as a tourist attraction. The various small booklets about the fortress which are now available provide a lot of information about the work of the Restoration Society, as well as giving detailed accounts of the siege of 1782 and the associated naval battle which took place in Basseterre Bay. Because of this, and because the sale of such literature assists in the upkeep of the fortress, nothing more about either the Society or the siege need be mentioned here.

The Prince of Wales bastion and the Parade Ground

The caretaker's house is about 400 feet above sea-level, which is only halfway up the hill. It is dominated by the wall of the **Magazine Bastion**, which protected the western and northern approaches. The narrow, paved road leads inside the fortress through an archway in this wall. Once inside it zig-zags upwards and through another archway on to a reasonably level piece of ground. This second archway is part of the **Prince of Wales Bastion**, which affords a bird's eye view of all the lower fortifications. It is well worth walking around before proceeding any higher. Another stretch of flat ground overlooks this bastion from between the twin peaks of Brimstone Hill. The lower of the two is a rounded elevation called **Monkey Hill**, while the true summit is occupied by the citadel. The flat ground, it goes without saying, used to be the **Parade Ground**; it is now a car park. The western side of the car park is bounded by the roof of a long narrow building which served as the quarters for the officers of whichever regiment was based in the fortress. The upper storey of this building (the 'roof' is in fact the first floor) has long since disappeared leaving one with the impression that, for some reason, the officers lived underground. In front of and well below the level of the parade ground is a large bowl-shaped area which acted as a water catchment for an enormous 100 000 gallon cistern. The slabs with which it was once paved have long since been carted away.

For anyone with a special interest in military history, Georgian architecture or military engineering there is much to be seen and explored away from the parade ground and the road leading up to it. There are several paths leading to the remoter parts of the fortress, and the enthusiast will undoubtedly find a great deal to interest him in areas ignored by the majority of visitors. The latter, having looked at the various numbered points of interest, will turn automatically towards the long flight of stone steps leading from the parade ground to the citadel.

Fort George

The citadel, **Fort George**, was named after King George III of England. It is a massive regular pentagon, with an equally substantial

Inside the fortress (MICHAEL BOURNE)

place of arms to the east and west of it, which dominated the entire fortress. The citadel, which is an open courtyard surrounded by barracks, is entered through a doorway at the western end. Once inside steps lead both down to the courtyard and up on to the gun platform which forms the roof of the barracks. Several of the barrack rooms have been converted into a museum, each one displaying a different aspect of the island's history. The exhibits, which range from pre-Columbian artefacts to mementoes of recent visits by members of the British royal family, are diverting and well-displayed. There is a certain amount of material about the construction of the fortress and its restoration, but surprisingly there is nothing whatever about a tragic accident which happened in the citadel itself only a generation or so ago.

For many years it was the custom for Kittitians to visit Brimstone Hill on Easter Monday for a picnic. On that day in 1950 something like two thousand people attended. Most of them were in the courtyard of the citadel, or on the western place of arms listening to the music of steel bands, when heavy rain swept down from the mountains behind the hill. In the ensuing mêlée produced by crowds from both the courtyard and the place of arms rushing for shelter through the citadel's single entrance, eleven people were trampled and suffocated. That this should have happened in a place designed as a refuge adds terrible irony to a dire tragedy. Since then no more Easter picnics have taken place, and the disaster is now all but forgotten.

While the museum is well worth a visit it does not provide the main reason for climbing up to the citadel. This has to be for the view from the top of the battlements, which is truly magnificent. Besides enabling nearly the whole of the western side of the island to be seen at a glance, it also takes in on a clear day the islands of Nevis, Sint Eustatius, Saba, St Martin and Saint-Barthélemy. The last, which is due north of St Kitts, can just be seen around the western slopes of Mt Liamuiga.

This mountain fills the rest of the horizon, dominating its volcanic offshoot just as Brimstone Hill itself dominates the coastal plain below. The hill was dubbed 'the Gibraltar of the Caribbean' long before tourism came to St Kitts, and for once such an analogy is not too inappropriate. Gibraltar and Brimstone Hill are not too dissimilar in appearance, both were heavily fortified, and both endured a famous siege. Fortunately there never came into existence a legend about the hill similar to the one about Britain losing Gibraltar if the Barbary apes ever die out. The vervet monkeys which are seen from time to time among the ruins of the Brimstone Hill fortress originate from Africa, as do the apes on Gibraltar, but that is as far as the resemblance goes.

| 12 |
Sandy Point to the Sugar Factory

The small town a mile or so to the north of Brimstone Hill is called **Sandy Point**. It is the largest community outside Basseterre but there is little other than its size to distinguish it from any other village. From Sandy Point the main road leads around the northern end of the island through what, in the seventeenth century, was called Capesterre. This is recalled in the names of two of the northern parishes, St Paul Capesterre and St John Capesterre, but otherwise the only other reminders of French days are Belle Tete, the westernmost point of the island, and Dieppe Bay near the northernmost point. The whole of this district, from the coast to a thousand feet above sea-level on the side of Mt Liamuiga, is covered with nothing but sugar-cane fields. Out of all the estates only two have some attraction for visitors.

Swimming pool at Rawlins Plantation (MICHAEL BOURNE)

Climbing to the crater

Belmont Estate, about three miles from Sandy Point, is the starting place for the climb up to the **crater of Mt Liamuiga**. This hike, which although not particularly difficult is long, hot and rough, is now a regular feature of the tourist scene. It is not something which should be attempted by solitary climbers. Day trips for small groups, with transport as far up the mountain as a cross-country vehicle can get, refreshments and a guide, are organised by several of the hotels and are recommended.

The crater is circular, about half a mile in diameter, and some 700 feet deep. The descent into it from the rim is very steep and can only be undertaken by holding on to creepers and vines, and getting dirty in the process. There is no true crater lake, but water does gather in the western part to a depth of a few feet underneath a cliff. Elsewhere there are a few sulphureous vents and at least one active soufrière with boiling water. Mt Liamuiga is a jagged pinnacle on the eastern side, rising in a sheer cliff some 1700 feet from the floor of the crater.

Estimates of the time needed to reach the rim of the crater from where the motorable track ends vary a great deal. A guide book written in the early 1900s mentions a two-hour 'walk' from the end of the cane fields. The same estimate is given in a similar book of the 1930s, adding 'all that is needed is a sound heart and a good wind'. A modern tourist guide states that a 'full day' must be allowed 'for this exciting excursion', while another authority mentions six hours as being required. However long it takes, and obviously it will depend on factors such as the state of the track, the size of the party, and the progress of the least fit member, the hike will add a memorable day to any vacation.

Two elegant hostelries

The tourists seen leaving Belmont estate having been up to the crater and back, perhaps slipping and sliding down a rain-sodden trail, will bear little resemblance to those who may be leaving the neighbouring estate of Mount Pleasant at the same time. The ruins of the estate works at Mount Pleasant have been restored and converted

The Golden Lemon Hotel (MICHAEL BOURNE)

into a small and extremely elegant hotel called **Rawlins Plantation**, set in the middle of some exceptionally well-kept gardens. The tower of a windmill and the ruins of an old molasses boiling house have been incorporated into the hotel, and even the works chimney has been made to appear ornamental. The setting of the hotel, now that every aspect of its former connection with the sugar industry has been transmogrified, is slightly incongruous in the middle of endless cane fields. But be that as it may, Rawlins Plantation is a charming place and worth a detour from the main road up a long and dusty track – even though this may mean having to pull into the side to let the cane tractors go by.

At **Dieppe Bay Town** there is another relic of former days which has been transformed out of all recognition. Dieppe Bay, which is no more than a hamlet, acquired its status as a 'town' from having been in existence since the days of Saint-Christophe. This part of the north coast is protected by a large coral reef a few hundred yards offshore, leaving just enough room between it and the shore to form

111

a shallow harbour. This was used in days gone by as a port for shipping sugar in small sailing vessels; today it gives shelter to a few fishing boats and the occasional yacht. A long stone sugar warehouse near the water's edge has been greatly restored and turned into the **Golden Lemon Hotel**. Its appointments and gardens are if anything even finer than those of Rawlins Plantation. Its setting, as a luxurious hotel squeezed between a rather drab village street and an equally dreary grey sand beach, is no less incongruous. Although it is most unlikely that the owner of either hotel would agree, or wish to use it in his advertising, the incompatibility of each establishment with its surroundings does in some way, peculiar to St Kitts, add to the charm and individuality of both.

Rocks and monkeys

The east coast, from Dieppe Bay Town to Cayon, is less interesting than the opposite side of the island. There are no historic sites, and little out of the ordinary – for St Kitts – in the scenery. The **'Black Rocks'** at **Belle Vue** are worth stopping to look at, but after that only a closed railway crossing need cause further delay. The rocks are the seaward end of a massive lava flow from Mt Liamuiga, the only such formation on the island. As the lava reached the sea however many millions of years ago it cooled and solidified into the grotesque shapes which now form cliffs along this part of the coast.

About two miles further on along the coast road an avenue of tall palm trees off to the right marks the approaches to **Estridge Estate**. The estate house has been converted into the field centre for the rather sinister sounding Behavioural Science Foundation. For some years, and for reasons which are not advertised and which are not clear to the layman, research has been carried on here into the 'social behaviour of the vervet monkey'. Although the official tourist brochures advocate visiting the place, casual callers are not welcome, and the animals whose behaviour is being studied are not shown to the public. The one or two monkeys to be seen in a crude cage near the field centre would appear to be those whose conduct is too anti-social to be worth recording, and put there to deter visitors.

Diver exploring the exotic 'Black Rocks' reef at
Belle Vue (opposite) (CHRIS HUXLEY)

The tourist, unless she is a zoologist, an anthropologist or a trustee of the research Foundation, should ignore both the advice in the tourist literature and the inviting avenue of trees leading to the Estridge Estate, and proceed for another three miles to the village of Ottley's. There she will find a warmer welcome at **Ottley's Plantation Inn**, half a mile or so above the village on the side of the mountain. This is another converted estate house, with superb appointments and equally superb views.

Fountain Estate and the 'stately Castle'

From the village of **Cayon** it is possible to return to Basseterre by two routes, either by following the low, coastal road to **Conaree** and around the airport, or by taking a higher secondary road across Greenhill and into the valley between Monkey Hill and the Canada Hills. The latter passes through the little villages of **Stapleton** and **St Peter's** before circling the western end of the airport and entering Basseterre. The high road is the more interesting, if a bit bumpier. At Stapleton, which is just over three miles north of the capital, a track off to the right of the road leads through the cane fields up the eastern side of Olivee's Mountain. At around a thousand feet above sea-level and maybe a mile from Stapleton is **Fountain Estate House**. This is built on the ruins of '**La Fontaine**', the residence erected in the 1640s by de Poincy, the Captain-General of Saint-Christophe. The present house, which is no longer connected with the surrounding sugar estate, of course bears no resemblance to the original. The cane fields which hem it in on every side make it very difficult to appreciate how the 'stately Castle' might have looked, or how its grounds were landscaped; they also obscure some of its outlying remains.

Facts about de Poincy's house are scarce. A contemporary engraving shows a four-square building of at least four storeys (it is not clear whether something on the flat roof is another room or some form of decoration) set in several acres of formal, walled gardens. It is hard to believe that this is anything more than a seventeenth century equivalent of the modern 'architect's impression' – a drawing using perspective and an incredible amount of artist's licence to portray, for the client, a building looking twice as big as the one which will be built. Remembering that the first French settlement dates from 1625 and that La Fontaine was erected some three miles from Basseterre at a height of one thousand feet on the side of a mountain less than twenty years later, makes it inconceivable that the house was anything like the Louis XIII style chateau depicted in the engraving. In any case, the actual topography bears no relationship to that in the picture, with very little level ground which would lend itself to being laid out as shown.

There is no doubt that a substantial gubernatorial residence was built on the site – there are enough remains, including the entrance tunnel to underground stables, to show that de Poincy lived in some style – but no proper investigation has ever been carried out. After it was rendered uninhabitable by the 1689 earthquake it was of course vandalised in the usual manner, and the subsequent construction of an estate house would have obscured the original ground plan. Even so, modern archaeologists and historians are able to reconstruct the past from the most fragmentary evidence, and the ruins of La Fontaine may still one day come into their own. Today it is hardly worth the effort of bumping up a long and dusty track to Fountain Estate to view that little that is visible. But who knows? – in years to come the remains of La Fontaine may well prove to be a prime tourist attraction, and for more than one reason. Even if he did not know how to build an earthquake-proof building, at least de Poincy knew how to choose a site with a view. A little over

The Sugar Factory (MICHAEL BOURNE)

a mile away, at St Peter's, yet another estate house has been restored and converted into a private hotel. **The White House** does not have quite as good a view as La Fontaine, but it more than makes up for this with ease of access and by its proximity to Basseterre.

Sugar again

Whether the final leg of the island tour is made by the low road or the high road it ends where these roads meet on the south side of the airport. It seems appropriate to end this chapter, and the tour, at this particular point – within a few hundred yards of the **Sugar Factory**. A conducted tour of the factory is not something which is a daily occurrence, but the management will gladly arrange one given a day or two's notice. On every side all around the island, surrounding each historic site and place of interest, there are cane fields which no visitor can fail to see. From the beginning of February, halfway through the 'tourist season', it is impossible for anyone travelling around the island not to be aware of the various activities associated with reaping the crop. To tour St Kitts is to tour the sugar estates. What could be more appropriate then but to complete the journey by touring the place where the cane is turned into raw sugar?

Epilogue

When reviewing the long list of disasters which have affected the island and its people, from the first recorded inhabitants onwards, it has to be admitted that history has been most unkind to St Kitts. Geography, on the other hand, has been very kind. It was the 'fertile island' to the Caribs, and it remained just that for the first settlers, for the 'plantocracy', and for the latter-day Sugar Growers' Association. It remains so today for the St Kitts Sugar Manufacturing Corporation, and it will continue to be so tomorrow for whatever new agricultural activities come along. Geography has also seen to it that the island is of such a character that the present moves towards diversifying the economy can proceed without any clash of interests.

Each of the three main aspects of the new economy falls neatly into one of three main topographical regions of the island. Sugar-cane is grown on the lower slopes of the mountains, industry is confined to the central low-lying areas around Basseterre, and the main tourist area is in the northern part of the south-eastern peninsula. Future developments in any one sector are going to take place in the same region. Any new agricultural activity will be started only at the expense of sugar-cane, using the same land. The most obvious place for new industries to be established is within easy reach of Basseterre, the airport and the harbour. The only potential for tourism development is along the peninsula, where the beaches are golden and the rainfall limited. This very convenient geographical sub-division is the most valuable factor in the economic future of St Kitts. It allows each sector of the economy to be developed without harming the others – something which is very rare in any country, let alone the small islands of the eastern Caribbean.

Although traumatic at the time the breaking away of Anguilla from the newly formed Associated State in 1967 was a blessing in disguise. The continued affiliation with six thousand disgruntled inhabitants of a very poor island nearly sixty miles away would have brought little benefit to either Anguillans or Kittitians. Getting rid of the

117

Boyd's Level Crossing (BRIAN DYDE)

Anguilla encumbrance probably assisted in concentrating people's minds on the relationship of St Kitts with Nevis. The present *modus vivendi* seems largely designed to allow both islands to be developed by their own citizens, with a minimum of interference from each other. Even if it does not last no harm need be occasioned to each other as a result. With or without Nevis, St Kitts seems well poised to cope with a future which promises to be very different from its past.

Just as the seventeenth century colony founded jointly by Warner and d'Esnambuc soon became a model for many others in the eastern Caribbean, so may the St Kitts of tomorrow turn out to be (no doubt, much to the surprise of some of the richer and at present more developed islands round about) the ideal example of the small independent island State of the twenty-first century.

MACMILLAN CARIBBEAN GUIDES SERIES
– Other titles available

Dyde: *Antigua & Barbuda: The Heart of the Caribbean*
Saunders: *The Bahamas: A Family of Islands*
Hoyos: *Barbados: The Visitor's Guide*
Raine: *The Islands of Bermuda: Another World*
Cutlack: *Belize: Ecotourism in Action*
Gravette: *Cuba: Official Guide*
Halabi: *Curaçao Close-Up*
Honychurch: *Dominica: Isle of Adventure*
Sinclair: *Grenada: Isle of Spice*
Dyde: *Islands to the Windward: Five Gems of the Caribbean* (St Maarten/St Martin, St Barts, St Eustatius, Saba, Anguilla)
Sherlock and Preston: *Jamaica: Fairest Isle: An Introduction and Guide*
Fergus: *Montserrat: Emerald Isle of the Caribbean*
Gordon: *Nevis: Queen of the Caribees*
Ellis: *St Lucia: Helen of the West Indies*
Sutty: *St Vincent and the Grenadines*
Taylor: *Trinidad and Tobago: A Guide and Introduction*
Smithers: *The Turks and Caicos Islands: Lands of Discovery*
Shepard: *The British Virgin Islands: Treasure Islands of the Caribbean*